Go to Galilee

A Travel Guide for Christian Pilgrims

Jacob Firsel

*"Go and tell my brothers to
go to Galilee;
there they will see me."*

Matthew 28:10

Go to Galilee: A Travel Guide for Christian Pilgrims
1st edition, May 2011

Text and photographs copyright © 2011 Jacob Firsel except front cover (see below) and p. 48, © Nazareth Village.

All Maps © Village to Village Press
Editing, layout and design by Village to Village Press
www.villagetovillagepress.com

Cover photographs: Front: Mt. Bereniki overlooking the Sea of Galilee © David Landis; Back: Mosaic at Tabgha © Jacob Firsel

ISBN 978-0-9843533-1-6
Library of Congress Control Number: 2011928733

TABLE OF CONTENTS

FOREWORD

This book is for those of you who want to come to the Holy Land and visit the places where Jesus walked. With book in hand, I want you to enjoy the experience and, hopefully, something deeper.

Most of my Christian friends say that they come away from the Holy Land changed. They read the Bible and truly understand places, events and personalities. It is one thing to read the Bible in Cleveland, Leeds or Cape Town and quite another to stand on the shores of the Sea of Galilee and hear "the Teacher's" words. I hope that this book will motivate those who have yet to walk in the paths of Jesus, entertain those who do and fill a much-needed niche aching to be filled.

I would like to thank my editors and publishers at Village to Village Press, Anna and David Landis for taking on this project. Kudos to Harry Adler, my good friend and colleague of many years, for proofreading the manuscript and last but not least, my wife Rivka, for putting up with me while working on this book.

God Bless,
Jacob Firsel

INTRODUCTION

Go to Galilee is a guidebook for Christian visitors to the northern region of the present State of Israel. The book is written from the perspective of a Jewish Israeli of American background about the most influential person in history.

Jesus was Jewish.[1] He was born of a Jewish mother and was raised in a Jewish village, following Jewish law and teachings (*Torah*), and was concerned about matters affecting his fellow Jews. He, his family, his neighbors and his disciples were Jews.

This book begins with Jesus' childhood home of Nazareth and moves to the place where he and his father probably spent a great deal of their time, Sepphoris (called Zippori in Hebrew). The book continues on to the village of Capernaum, Jesus' home base during his ministry, and then on to the various sites in the Galilee where Jesus taught, performed miracles and eventually changed the world. As you follow Jesus' footsteps through his ministry in Galilee, remember that he was both a genius and a revolutionary.

Judaism was anything but simple during his lifetime. Scholars have identified four main sects of first-century Judaism:

1. **Pharisees** or scribes, who came mainly from the common people and believed in the Oral Law (biblical interpretation of the Hebrew Bible) as well as maintaining the Temple cult in Jerusalem. They believed in life after death and an end of days in which a messiah would defeat foreign rule and establish a kingdom of God.

---

1   The term "Jew" derives from the geographical region known as Judea, where the tribe of Judah settled (Joshua 15:1-4).

2. **Sadducees**, who were made up of the aristocratic priestly families and did not believe in any interpretation of the Bible. They did not believe in an afterlife and were only concerned with the Temple cult in Jerusalem.

3. **Essenes,** who were made up mostly of dissident priests from Jerusalem. They opposed the corrupt priests ruling in Jerusalem and retreated to the desert at Qumran to await the final war between the sons of light (these being themselves, the Essenes) and the sons of darkness (everybody else, especially the Romans). They were wiped out in the Jewish Revolt against Rome which ended with the destruction of Qumran in the year 69 CE.

4. **Zealots**, who were made up of fanatic religious extremists who did not accept any foreign rule in the land of Israel. Called Sicarii (literally "daggermen,") by the first-century Jewish historian Josephus, they would conceal sharp daggers in their cloaks and assassinate political opponents in crowds and then melt away into the masses. The Zealots disappear from history with the fall of Masada in the year 73 CE.

THE JEWISH JESUS

Jesus is a Greek translation of the Hebrew name *Yeshua*. Yeshua is a Galilean pronunciation of the name Joshua. This is no accident. Pronounced *Yehoshua* in Hebrew, the name means redeemer or deliverer. Christ (Christos) is Greek for messiah. Messiah is taken from the Hebrew work *Mashuach*, literally meaning "anointed one."

Jesus was probably born in the year 7 BCE[2] in Bethlehem in Judea. He spent most of his life in Nazareth, but also spent a good deal of time in Jerusalem and, of course, the last three years of his life he

---

2   BCE (Before the Common Era) or BC; CE used for Common Era or AD

spent in and around the holy triangle of Galilee between the towns of Capernaum, Korazim and Bethsaida. To the Jewish population of the Galilee, Jesus was a popular rabbi who performed miracles and differed from the Pharisees in that he taught in parables.

Jesus was very aware of the law and its proscriptions. He always said a blessing before eating (like Orthodox Jews today) and even goes as far to say that he will not destroy the law, but rather fulfill it (Matthew 5:17).

THE GALILEE

The Galilee is a region in northern Israel. The name comes from the Hebrew root *Galil* which means "round" or "circular," referring to the rolling hills or mountains and the valleys between them. The first-century Jewish historian Flavius Josephus wrote that the word meant "district."

Bordered by the Beit Shean Valley to the south, the Jordan Valley to the east, Lebanon to the north and the Coastal Plain in the west, Galilee was the heartland of the breakaway Kingdom of Israel which "seceded from the union," as it were, when the ten northern tribes broke away from the Davidic line's successor Rehoboam (his tribe, Judah, and the tribe of Benjamin stayed loyal) under the leadership of Jeraboam in the year 933 BCE. The Northern Kingdom became the stronger of the two until its destruction in the year 722 BCE by the the Assyrians under king Sargon II.

The Assyrians exiled conquered peoples to remote parts of their empire and, in turn, peopled those areas with others from their empire's interior. The ten northern tribes were scattered to the winds and disappeared from history (until recently when people, claiming to be descendants of the lost ten tribes, are turning up from India to Africa). Pagan newcomers were settled in the Galilee.

When Judea fell to the Babylonians in 586 BCE, the southerners were taken from the land of Israel, but returned two generations later in the year 538 BCE. The walls around Jerusalem were rebuilt under the leadership of the prophet Ezra in the year 435 BCE.

There was a clear distinction between Galileans (northerners) and Judeans (southerners). As in the United States a century ago, both sides viewed each other with more than suspicion. Galileans spoke with an accent (see Matt 26:73) and were seen as lax in ritual observances, but were zealous of their freedom from foreign oppression. Indeed, a good number of the most extreme rebels in the Jewish Revolt against Rome were Galileans.

I imagine that during the three Jewish festivals— Passover, Pentecost (Shavu'oth) and the Feast of Tabernacles (Succoth), when Jews from all over the land of Israel went up to Jerusalem, the Galileans may have been considered unsophisticated by the street-wise Jerusalemites.

The Galileans were mostly farmers and simple day laborers. Many of them came from families that had been forcibly converted by the Jewish King Alexander Yannai at the end of the 2nd century BCE. Alexander added large parts to his kingdom and gave the inhabitants a choice: convert to Judaism or leave. Like many new converts, they and their sons were zealous in their belief in God and in his redemption of the Jewish people.

The Galilee was a hotbed of rebellion for hard-working, God-fearing, no-nonsense folk who truly thought the kingdom of God and freedom from the Roman chokehold was just around the corner.

JESUS OF NAZARETH, GALILEAN CELEBRITY

A recent television production portrayed Jesus walking into a small town market square in Galilee. He choses a spot, climbs up on a convenient rock and begins to speak. Gradually a few passersby stop and listen.

This is a popularly-held misconception. Jesus was very well known, not only to the locals in Galilee, but all over the land. Matthew tells us that "News about him spread all over Syria, and people brought to him all who were ill..." (Matthew 4:24a). "Large crowds from Galilee, the Decapolis, Jerusalem, Judea and the region across the Jordan followed him" (Matthew 4:25).

Jesus was a celebrity! Not only in Galilee and Jerusalem, but also throughout the broader region, including present-day Lebanon, Jordan, Syria and the Palestinian Territories. Were he to head to any town in the region, word would spread and the sick in heart as well as body would be eagerly awaiting him.

Since his crucifixion and resurrection in about the year 30 CE, Jesus of Nazareth just may be the most influential person in the world.

This guide is intended for those who would like to not only visit the sites of his home and ministry, but experience first hand the towns and villages, mountains and valleys that shaped this most extraordinary man's world view.

I invite you to join me and go to Galilee to meet him.

The modern city of Nazareth, located in the lower Galilee.

Nazareth

Jesus' Childhood Home

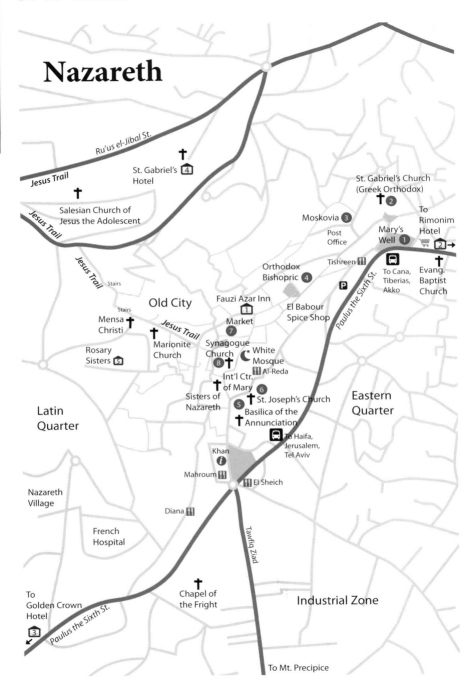

Nazareth

Ru'us el-Jibal St.

Jesus Trail

St. Gabriel's Hotel ✝ ⌂ 4

St. Gabriel's Church (Greek Orthodox) ✝ ⌂ 2

To Rimonim Hotel

Jesus Trail

Salesian Church of Jesus the Adolescent ✝

Moskovia 3

Mary's Well 1 🛒 ⌂ 2 →

Post Office

Jesus Trail

Stairs

Tishreen 🍴

🅿

To Cana, Tiberias, Akko 🚌

Evang. Baptist Church ✝

Orthodox Bishopric 4

Old City

Stairs

Fauzi Azar Inn 1 ⌂

El Babour Spice Shop

Paulus the Sixth St.

Mensa Christi ✝

Market 7

Jesus Trail

Rosary Sisters 5 ⌂

Marionite Church ✝

Synagogue Church 8 ✝

White Mosque ☾ *

Al-Reda 🍴

Int'l Ctr. of Mary ✝

Eastern Quarter

Latin Quarter

Sisters of Nazareth

5 ✝ St. Joseph's Church ✝ 6

Basilica of the Annunciation ✝

🚌 To Haifa, Jerusalem, Tel Aviv

Khan ℹ

Mahroum 🍴

El Sheich 🍴

Nazareth Village

Diana 🍴

French Hospital

Tawfiq Ziad

To Golden Crown Hotel ⌂ 3 ↙

Chapel of the Fright ✝

Industrial Zone

Paulus the Sixth St.

To Mt. Precipice

TOUR 1 SNAPSHOT

Sites
Latin (Catholic) Basilica of the Annunciation, Market (Souk), Synagogue Church, Orthodox Church of the Annunciation and Mary's Well are the minimum. Add a tour of Nazareth Village and a meal or two with a night at the Fauzi Azar Inn to complete the day.

Length of Visit
Plan to spend at least a day here.

Type of Tour
Walking

Additional Highlights
A walk or short drive to Mount Precipice could begin day two before delving deeper into what Nazareth has to offer.

How to Get to Nazareth
Bus
From Tel Aviv: **Bus 823,** Tel Aviv Central Bus Station to Nazareth, 2 hr 40 min, (112 km), runs from 5:30am to 4:55pm, 5 times a day. Cost: 42NIS. Get off at city center (Basilica of the Annunciation). **Sheruts** (see p. 181) leave regularly from outside the Tel Aviv bus station. Sheruts are faster and run on Shabbat.

From Jerusalem: **Bus 955,** Jerusalem Central Bus Station to Nazareth, 4pm and 6 pm on weekdays, 2 hours, 48NIS.

From Tiberias: **Bus 431,** leaves hourly, 45 min, 20NIS.

From Haifa: **Bus 331,** leaves hourly from the Haifa Bay Bus Station (Merkezet Hamifratz, next to the train station located in the Cinemall), 45 min- 1 hr, 15.50NIS.

TOUR 1 INTRODUCTION

Jesus spent most of his life in this small country village in the mountains. At around the age of thirty, Jesus left his hometown and went northeast to the rich, fertile valleys surrounding the Sea of Galilee. However, Jesus is a product of Nazareth. This agricultural village set in the mountains of the lower Galilee greatly influenced him and his teaching.

Jesus' hometown today is a sprawling city of 72,000 Muslims and Christians with another 42,000 in neighboring mostly Jewish Upper Nazareth. Nazareth has to its credit the largest church in the Middle East, great little hotels and bed and breakfasts, restaurants that range from falafel in pita bread to quality restaurants with finicky chefs.

Unfortunately, many Christian tour groups spend only an hour or two in this great city and a few will suffice with a drive by.

This is a great pity. Nazareth is truly a great tourist city which deserves at least a day of your trip in the Holy Land.

I invite you not only to visit the churches, but to walk the streets, smell the smells and savor the taste of what Nazareth has to offer.

Mary's Well, once the center of the small village of Nazareth.

From Afula: Afula is a small town just south of Nazareth. The bus station here is a main hub for traveling north. **Bus 955, 823 and 355** run regularly to Nazareth.

Train
No train service available direct to Nazareth. From Tel Aviv or Beer Sheva you can take a train to Haifa (station Merkezet Hamifratz or Hashmona) and take the 331 bus to Nazareth. Train schedules at http://www.rail.co.il/EN.

How to get around Nazareth
Bus service, cabs, and car rental agencies are available in the city. However, if you have a car, I recommend leaving it either at Mary's Well or in one of the car parks just off the main rotary in front of the Basilica of the Annunciation and walking most of the tour.

The tour begins at Mary's Well Square in the middle of the Arab city of Nazareth on Paul VI Street, the main artery of the city.

1. MARY'S WELL SQUARE

The lovely arched fountain of Mary's Well, called *Ein Sittna Miriam* in Arabic, is dry now but serves as a good place to begin the tour of Nazareth. Water from the three ancient springs at the bottom of *Jebel esh-Sheikh* (Arabic for "hill of the Lord," known in English as Mt. Hermon) are brought to the Greek Orthodox Church of the Annunciation and then piped here. When the well underwent restoration in 1956, the water didn't make it here as the square was built above the water flow. Called a *Sabeel* in Arabic, the fountain has served the residents of Nazareth since 1862, and was rededicated in 1911. A large pool was located where the large ficus tree stands today. In the past, the pool helped irrigate small farms nearby.

In ancient times, this would have been the center of the small village. This was the place where the women of Nazareth would gossip as they fetched water (Bringing water was then considered "women's work.") Perhaps here is where the angel Gabriel met Mary and asked her to be the mother of Jesus. The Orthodox Church remembers this event as happening near the well.

To the right of the well is the **Cactus Gift Shop** (☎04-657-8539; 9am-7pm Mon-Sat, www.nazarethbathhouse.org). Owner Elias Shama sells jewelry and souvenirs there, but underneath his establishment are preserved remnants of a bathhouse, which Shama claims is 2,000 years old. However, most experts date it much later. A tour is 120NIS for a group; no individual prices.

Walk up the stairs behind the well to the church on the square.

2. ST. GABRIEL'S ORTHODOX CHURCH OF THE ANNUNCIATION

7am-6pm daily ☎*04-657-6437*

Sometimes referred to as the Church of St. Gabriel, this building was constructed in 1750 CE atop an older Crusader chapel which commemorates the annunciation according to the Orthodox tradition. This tradition is based on the "Gospel According to James" or "Protoevangelium of James," a 2nd century CE document which places the meeting of Mary and the angel Gabriel at the well.

The Crusader church, along with the other Christian structures in the city, was destroyed by the Mamluk general Baibars in 1263 CE.

The church measures 14x14 m (46x46 ft, square churches are common in the Orthodox rite) and built of native limestone. Upon entering the church, note the beautiful paintings on the walls. Created by the Romanian artists Michel and Gabriel Marosan in 1977-78, the works depict scenes from the Old and New Testaments. The splendid hand-carved wooden *iconostasis* (the screen in Orthodox churches separating the priest from the worshippers), a gift from a Greek merchant, was installed in 1767 by Adrian Maistu.

Church Etiquette

This is a good time to lay down some ground rules for visiting churches in the Middle East. Men should uncover their heads and trousers/pants should be worn. No shorts, please! Women should have their shoulders and knees well-concealed. When sitting in an Orthodox church, never cross your legs! Foot is a four-letter word in the Holy Land! Seeing the bottom of someone's feet is considered profane. Really.

St. Gabriel's Orthodox Church of the Annunciation, near Mary's Well in Nazareth.

CATHOLIC VS. ORTHODOX

We meet here for the first time the "rivalry" between the two main sects of Christianity in this part of the world: the Catholic and Orthodox churches. This has its roots in the schism of the 11th century and the Crusades. Often at important sites in the Holy Land, there will be two churches: one Catholic, called "Latin" in the Middle East (until 1964, the language of the mass was Latin); the other Orthodox, whose center was Constantinople, today's Istanbul in Turkey.

Directly opposite the entrance is the Crusader crypt. This is one of the oldest surviving religious constructions in Nazareth. Once part of the Crusader church, the crypt marks the holiest place for many visitors. On the left (upon descending) is water for pilgrims taken from the well. This water is believed to have medicinal properties.

There is no admission fee for visiting the church, but it is considered polite is to leave a few shekels in the offering.

Leave the church gate and follow the road right as it curves away from the church. Walk about 30m until you come to a large white building. Here stands part of a compound called the Moskovia.

3. THE MOSKOVIA

(The main building is closed, but you can walk around to the right to peek inside the courtyard, which today serves as a parking lot).

This large building is actually part of a complex built in 1904 to host Russian pilgrims. As the sign says, "1,000 at a time could sleep here." The complex boasted a hospital, pharmacy, and school. There is a modern post office here in case you need stamps (post offices in Israel are the best place to change currency as they take no fee!). The Moskovia housed the district court until a new one was built in nearby Nazareth Illit, a Jewish development town.

The "Moskovia" - a remnant of the Russian Empire

Development Towns

"Development town" is a term used to describe a community where the Israeli government settled new immigrants who poured into the state in the 1950s and 60s. They were usually established in the peripheral areas in the North and South of the country. Complete infrastructures were built in the space of just a few years to accommodate the influx of newcomers, most of whom were from North Africa and Eastern Europe.

Continue walking into the Old City from the Moskovia. Pass the Orthodox Bishopric on the right. Note the granite columns on either side of the entrance. On the door itself is the "taphos"—the Greek letters that designate ownership by the Orthodox Church. Arrive at Bishop's Square in front of the "Writer's House" and "Orthodox Bishopric."

4. ORTHODOX BISHOPRIC, HOME OF MARY AND JOSEPH AND MARTYRS' CAVE

9-11:30am Mon-Sat

A green wrought-iron gate leads to the Orthodox Bishopric of Nazareth. If locked, ring the bell and someone will come shortly from the offices to the right. A later Orthodox tradition places the home of Mary and Joseph (and his carpentry shop) here, closer to the well.

Walking through the courtyard, you are led to another gate which winds left down into a cave. The cave is simple and has a few altars. The priests tell of a massacre of 40 martyrs, probably when Crusader Nazareth was destroyed by Baibars in 1263. Interesting and seldom visited, the shrine exudes a somber holiness not often found in Galilee.

PROPER PEDESTRIAN BEHAVIOR

It is always a good idea to walk on the left side of the road, against traffic. Streets are narrow in many old cities in the Middle East and drivers can see you better. Drivers in Israel have a well-deserved reputation for recklessness. One-third of all traffic fatalities are pedestrians! Heads up and eyes open!

Upon leaving the Bishopric, look right to the "Writer's House," a fine example of a 19th-century Arab merchant's home. The easiest way to the next stop, the Basilica of the Annunciation, is to go back to the Moskovia and descend on the lower street. As you descend, you will see a sign for the restaurant "Tishreen." Turn right here and follow Annunciation Street (*Bishara* street in Arabic). You will notice the steeples of St. Joseph's Church and the Basilica.

Note the large Muslim cemetery on the right. Continue past St. Joseph's school on your left. Pass the first entrance to the Basilica here on your left, keeping to the sidewalk. Pass the entrance to the market on the right (you will return and visit the shuk later in the tour) and turn left. On your left will be the office of the Basilica complex where you can get information about the site. The entrance to the church is just 3 m (10 ft) ahead.

5. BASILICA OF THE ANNUNCIATION

☎ *04-657-6437*

Upper church *open daily from 8am to 6pm;* **Lower church** *open daily from 5:30am to 6pm & for silent prayer from 6 - 9pm; Sundays from 12 noon to 6pm. Candlelight procession Saturdays 8:30pm.*

The largest church in the Middle East, the Basilica of the Annunciation, should be enjoyed slowly. Not only one of the most important religious edifices in the world, the Basilica is also a cornucopia of history, art and archaeology.

Construction began in 1960 after a meticulous excavation of the site by Franciscan archaeologist Father Bellarmino Bagatti in the 1950s in which mosaics from an earlier Byzantine church were found as well as walls of a much larger Crusader church from the 12th century. Remains from both of these churches were incorporated into the 20th-century basilica. There also was a small Franciscan church built on the site in 1730, which was expanded in 1870 and torn down (except for the grotto) in the 1950s to make way for the new basilica.

The architect, Professor Giovanni Muzio of Milan, designed the building to be large: 65 m (213 ft) long, 27 m (89 ft) wide, and 55 m (180 ft) high. The design was so big that Israeli civil engineering company Solel Boneh had to be called in for nine years of construction.

As you pass through the entrance gate, the gatekeeper will greet you (and ensure that you are appropriately attired). Don't enter the church just yet. Stand as far back as you can from the entrance to the basilica and look up.

The Basilica of the Annunciation in Nazareth. The steeple is reminiscent of a crown.

CHURCH PHASES

Most Christian holy sites in Israel are marked with churches. Most churches have three phases: Byzantine, Crusader and modern. Places like Mt. Tabor, Nazareth and Jerusalem have modern churches built on the ruins. Most Byzantine churces were destroyed by the Parthian (Persian) invasion of 614 CE.

"Byzantine" refers to the period from 325 CE to 638 CE. The word derives from "Byzantium," the capital city of the Eastern Roman Empire, today's Istanbul. Constantine I, the first Roman emperor to embrace Christianity, and especially his mother, Helena, declared many of the biblical sites as holy sites and opened the region for Christian pilgrimage.

Looking now at the western façade, a 3 m (10 ft) tall bronze statue of Christ is giving his blessing. Below, the angel Gabriel on the left and the Virgin Mary on the right are carved into the limestone. The Latin caption below them translates: "The angel of God spoke unto Mary." Underneath sit the four evangelists (Matthew, Mark, Luke and John) with their symbols: the angel, the lion, the ox and the eagle. To the right of the evangelists is a Latin quotation from the Hebrew Bible: "And the Lord God said unto the serpent... it shall bruise thy head and thou shalt bruise his heel" (Genesis 3:15). On the left, "Behold, a virgin shall conceive and bear a son, and shall call his name Immanuel" (Isaiah 7:14).

Most of the Byzantine churches destroyed in the early 7th century by the Parthians (from present-day Iran) were rebuilt by the Crusaders in the 12th and 13th centuries, only to be mostly destroyed again by the Mamluks after 1265 CE. The modern phase began from the middle of the 19th century, when the Ottoman

The Fransiscan Order

The Franciscan Order (OFM) was started by St. Francis of Assisi in the early 13th century and was named the custodian of the Holy Land (Custodia Terrae Santae), which made the Franciscans responsible for the upkeep and protection of sites holy to the Christian faith in the Holy Land. Whenever you see the Franciscan symbol (see text below), the site is in the hands of the Franciscans and, of course, the Roman Catholic Church.

Empire wooed European countries, offering *firmans* (special permits) signed by the Sultan himself granting permission to build churches and giving the property to the Catholic or Orthodox churches.

The Latin quotation under the carvings of the evangelists is from John 1:14, "And the word was made flesh, and dwelt among us."

Look at the pink bands of limestone that run horizontally along the façade. The first one with writing on it has stars on it representing air. The second band with writing has flames carved into it representing fire. The next bands below has fish in the element of water. Flowers and plants (representing earth) are underneath. Together, the four bands represent the four elements: air, fire, water and earth. This is an allusion to the four firmaments of heaven Jesus needed to cross to come to man.

Look at the doorway and note the on porphyry granite architrave (lintel) what looks like a letter "P" superimposed on the letter "X." These are Greek letters. The "P" is the Greek letter rho. The "X" is the letter kai. The "kai-rho" represents the first two letters in the Greek word *"christos"*— Christ.

On the left of the door are two bronze crossed arms on a globe. Between them, the five crosses of the "Jerusalem" or "Cosmic" Cross. This is the symbol of the Franciscan Order.

Now is a good time to look around the courtyard. The portico that surrounds the church is decorated with mosaics, statues and shrines dedicated to the Virgin Mary from all over the world.

Returning to the front of the church, notice the two large double doors. There are single doors to the left and right. These four doors are the work of German artist Roland Fredrichson. The central double doors are cast bronze and wrought copper. They depict 16 scenes of Jesus' life.

Starting at the top left, we see the angel heralding the birth of the messiah[1] and the shepherds in the field of Bethlehem. On the next panel, the Holy Family is in the manger with the ox and donkey looking on; under this to their left, the adoration of the Magi and the gifts of frankincense, gold and myrrh.[2]

To the right is the "Presentation at the Temple" (Luke 2:22-39). According to Jewish law, the "first fruits" of a women's womb (if that "first fruit" was a male child) would have to be brought to the Temple in Jerusalem forty days after the birth and a proper sacrifice given to redeem him. Two doves would be purchased by the family and sacrificed by the priests there.

Today, among Sabbath-observant Jews, this tradition has evolved into a ceremony called the *"pedaiyon."* If the women's firstborn is a boy, the family goes to someone of priestly descent (*Cohen* means priest in Hebrew, so most men named Cohen are descendants of the 24 extended families of priests who serviced the Temple in

---

1   Messiah really means "anointed one," a king who is anointed by having olive oil poured on his head by a prophet ("Then Samuel took a vial of oil, and pour it upon his head..." 1 Samuel 10:1).

2   The choice of these gifts was no accident. The three most valuable luxuries in the ancient world were gold, frankincense and myrrh. Why frankincense and myrrh? Burnt as incense, they covered the ever-present bad smells in cities back then. Frankincense was especially effective to cover the stench of death.

The bronze doors of the Basilica by Ronald Fredrichson

Jerusalem 2,000 years ago), pays a symbolic sum of money (which will go to charity), and the priest will bless the child.

Under the nativity is the "Flight to Egypt" (Matthew 2:13-23) and to the left, the "Massacre of the Innocents" (Matthew 2:16-18). On the bottom left, note Jesus learning from Joseph. To the left of this, Jesus as a 12-year-old, astonishing the scribes at the Temple in Jerusalem (Luke 2: 46-47).

On the right door on the bottom you will see Jesus being baptized by John in the Jordan River (Matthew 3:13; John 1:30). On the right hand bottom is Jesus raising the widow's dead son in Nain (Luke 7:11-15).

Above this we see Jesus spreading the good news, perhaps the scene of the Sermon on the Mount (Matthew 5: 2-9). A fishing boat bobs on the Sea of Galilee to its left.

Above this we see the Crucifixion, John and the Virgin to the left. On the right, the empty tomb, "He is not here; he is risen" (Luke 24:6). On the top, as he ascends to heaven, he takes the just with him who died before him.

The baptism in the Jordan

Sea of Galilee

The Sea of Galilee is really a lake. In Hebrew it's called Lake Kinneret. In the Gospels, it is also called Lake Genneserat (Luke 5) or "Sea of Tiberias" in John. Kinneret derives from the Hebrew word "harp," denoting the shape of this body of water.

The Courtyard of Mary

The red porphyry granite surrounding the doors shows the prophets and patriarchs on the left and the apostles on the right.

Look to the door on your left. It is called Prototypes of the Redemption—scenes from the Hebrew Bible starting with Adam and Eve aspiring to be gods on the top and their fall from grace into sweat and work and pain of childbirth. Note Noah's Ark and rainbow and the binding of Isaac at the bottom. The door on the right (west) represents prophesies of redemption.

If you have some time, don't enter the church just yet. Turn around and walk around the courtyard to the left.

This courtyard is dedicated to the Adoration of Mary. The bronze doors here depict twelve scenes in her life from her birth to the fulfillment of the protection of the faithful. The doors are the work of American sculptor F. Shrady.

Walk back to the church and enter through the door on the right.

The Basilica of the Annunciation has three levels: 1) the Grotto; 2) the Lower Church; and 3) the Upper Church. As you enter the Lower Church, notice that this part of the basilica is made of plain poured concrete. Light enters from the side from stained glass windows. To the left, you will see Crusader masonry. This is what remains of the 12th-century church now incorporated into the present structure. Continue to the left to see a railing surrounding the lower part. This is the grotto.

The grotto is what remains of the traditional site of the house of Mary and Joseph. What appears to be a cave is probably the cellar of a 1st-century CE home. Cellars were very important in this part of the world at that time as there was no refrigeration. Foods were kept down here to keep them from spoiling. Also, bell-shaped structures were carved into the limestone, plastered over and used

Entering the Basilica, the main part of the church leads you to the grotto.

as water cisterns. Cisterns were vital necessities, given the lengthy dry season in the region.

Standing at the railing, look down at the mosaics from older Byzantine buildings found on this site and the outline of an ancient apse[3] from the first level of church building here.

Looking upward, light pours in through an *oculus* situated in the Upper Church.

Down in front of you (to the right), note what seems to be either a baptismal pool or a Jewish immersion pool (mikvah). To the right is a mosaic with a cross and geometric designs.

---

3   From the Latin apsis "vault" or "arch"; usually a half-circular construction at the end of a building with a vaulted roof.

The Grotto behind the altar

Mikvah

Mikvahs were very important in the time of Jesus. Ritual purity 2,000 years ago meant being in a non-polluted state of holiness. Contact with impure things such as unclean animals, death, or blood rendered one in an impure state. A mikvah cleansed and enabled the worshipper to go and worship at the Temple in Jerusalem.

If open (no Mass being performed) walk down into the grotto. In front of you is a modern altar with a cave behind. Beyond the iron grate is the altar from the 18th-century shrine. Keep on walking around, go through the gate and walk down the steps for a closer look. As you pass the grotto, look at the mosaic behind the iron gate to your right. Written in Greek from the Byzantine era (313 CE to 638 CE) it reads, *"From Canon, Deacon of Jerusalem."*

As you walk back to the entrance, notice the Crusader walls to your left which stretch the entire length of the church. This gives some idea of how large the church was back then.

Follow the signs to get to the upper church.

After ascending a circular staircase, enter the upper level. Nothing prepares you for the church's sheer size and beauty. Some 65.5 m long, 26 m wide, and 46 m high at the top of the dome (200x80x150 ft), the structure is quite impressive.

A large mosaic covers the wall behind the high altar. Representing the second Vatican Council, it shows Jesus and St. Peter in the center with Mary on a throne beside them. Five popes from the 20th century (the latest one being Paul the VI) and martyrs, scholars, lay people surround them.

The wall of the 12th-century Crusader church preserved inside today's basilica

Directly to the left of the stairs is a colorful stained glass window by the French artist Max Ingrand. Notice the *fleurs-de-lis* on the bottom. This flower, which represents medieval France, is also the Madonna Lily that grows in Israel.

Moving ahead look on either side of the nave for representations of the Virgin Mary from 20 countries. Starting with **France** (that's the Cathedral at Chartres on the bottom) and moving on to **Canada** with Mary as a First Nations person in a field of terracotta.

The **Japanese** mosaic displays Mary in a kimono reserved for the royal family. Her hairstyle is that of a virgin. The baby Jesus also wears a kimono reserved for Japanese royalty. Note that Christians represent about 7% of the population of Japan.

Further down, **Mexico's** mosaic shows Our Lady of Guadeloupe. Note the conquistador and Indian shepherd who represent the Mexican peoples' heritage.

Australia's somber virgin and angel seem to be in mourning. The southern cross on the top, Mount Kosciusko and two lyre birds on the bottom make it clear that this is Australian.

Past the iron gate (which separates the main part of the church from the altar area) is **Lebanon's** contributions with the famous cedars of Lebanon and statue of Mary on Mount Harissa.
Further down, **Argentina's** mosaic shows the tree where Mary of Lujan is venerated. Lastly, the mosaic from the **UK** depicts the Chapel of Our Lady of Walsingham.

Because of the special relationship between Italy and the Vatican, **Italy** has two mosaics on either side of the altar.

The mosaic representing Japan depicts Jesus in a royal kimono.

Before moving on to the mosaics on the southern wall, walk to the center of the church under the copula and look up.

Striking in its beauty, the interior of the copula represents an inverted lily. There are 32x23 "M"s. In Jewish numerology, 32 represents God. Reversed, 23 could mean man created in God's image. The M could stand for either Mary or Messiah.

The sixteen stained glass windows represent the 12 apostles (note Judas kissing Jesus and Peter holding the keys to the kingdom). The others represent Mary's parents, Anne and Joachim, St. Ephraim the Syrian and St. Bernard of Clairvaux.

Like all Catholic churches, the Stations of the Cross are on the eight columns that support the copula. The glazed ceramics are the work of artist Angelo Biancini (1911-1988) of Italy. Captions are in Arabic.

The floor in front is inlaid with colored marble which tells of eight themes of Mary (for more detailed information, an excellent guidebook, *The Basilica in Nazareth* by Gumbert Ludwin, is sold next to the entrance of the Church).

Notice the marble inlays on the floor in the central nave. It conceals a number of birds ranging from the dove to a peacock. The dove, of course, represents the Holy Ghost and peace.

Looking over to the right, we see the marvelous mosaic of **Cameroon**. On the bottom is written "From beyond the rivers of Ethiopia they shall bring gifts" (Zeph 3:10).

Hungary shows the Queen of Hungary with St. Stephan's crown.

Behind the glass door are more international mosaics: A wooden representation of Mother and Child in royal **Chinese** attire and

Czech Republic's Mary mosaic displaying in the courtyard.

next to it, the newest addition to the Basilica, the Queen of **India** and an icon representing the local Greek Catholic community in Nazareth. Above the door is a carved wood mother and child from **Venezuela.**

Next **Brazil** honors the miracle of Paraiba, when in 1717 fishermen caught halves of a statue of the Madonna in their net. **Poland's** contribution shows the Black Madonna of Częstochowa above seven figures representing the Polish people at different times in their history.

Coming to the **United States**, artist Charles Madden has welded together more than 1,000 pieces of stainless steel and plated them with silver to make Mary's dress. Her face and hands are in gold over a background of baked enamel.

Portugal commemorates Our Lady of Fatima and the miracle of the sun in 1917, in which up to 100,000 witnessed a mass solar irregularity. **Spain** depicts St. James in pilgrim dress at Saragossa.

Exit the Upper Church by the door between the Canadian and Japanese mosaic. Walk a short distance to the baptistery on the right.

Looking over the railing, we see the archaeological remains of the 1st-century village of Nazareth (mainly underground silos, cisterns and storage pits).

Spain's St. James in pilgrim garb.

Walk straight up the stairs. There is a restroom here available for a small fee. Before going to the Church of St. Joseph, look at the Franciscan Monastery completed in 1930 that sits between the two churches. In the beautiful garden are statues and the remains of stone columns, bases, and capitals of earlier churches on this site.

If with a group, prearrange a visit to the museum situated under the courtyard where we stand. A 50NIS fee is charged for a group of 1 to 10 persons. The museum is worth a visit to see the Crusader-age capitals and ancient graffiti carved by early pilgrims.

Museum Hours are 8am-11:30am; 2pm-5pm daily; closed Sunday.

American artist Madden's "Immaculate Conception" in the Upper Basilica (opposite).

6. CHURCH OF ST. JOSEPH

Daily: 9-11:45am; 2-5pm, Sundays: 2-5pm

The Church of St. Joseph was completed in 1911, before the beginning of World War I. Architect Fr. Hinterkueser of Germany built the structure over a 12th-century Crusader church, taking care to keep to the Crusader lines by incorporating three apses into the modern church.

Upon entering the church, take the staircase to the right and go down to the crypt.

To the right, note what may be the remains of a Byzantine baptism basin. Having seven steps and covered with a simple mosaic, this basin probably served as a place where new members were baptized. The initiate stood in the circular depression on the upper right-hand side. The priest conducted the ceremony standing on the stone in front. Note that the person to be baptized would have been standing, no full immersion here.

Jesus and Mary comfort Joseph on his deathbed.

ST. JOSEPH, THE TECTON

Joseph never speaks in Scripture. He is mentioned a few times: the flight to Egypt, going to Bethlehem for the census, etc. He is remembered as a carpenter and described in the earliest Bibles written in Greek as a *tekton*. *Tekton* means builder. Not only did he work in wood, but probably also knew to carve stone, work in metal and, most importantly, knew to read and write and had a rudimentary knowledge of math. In the small villages of the Galilee where there was no local Rabbi, the *tecton* was often referred to by the locals on questions of Jewish law. Did Joseph tutor the young Jesus not only in his trade but also in Torah?

The rest of the crypt is honeycombed with ancient cisterns and storage pits. Be sure to turn around and note the three stained glass windows above the altars.

The first one on the right shows the angel Gabriel telling a dreaming Joseph not to divorce his new wife, but to give a home to Jesus (Matthew 1:18-25). The second one, in the middle, shows the scene of the marriage ceremony of Mary and Joseph. On the left, a dying Joseph is being comforted by Mary and Jesus. These striking windows are the work of S. Gruber of Strasbourg. Going back up the stairs, note the stained glass window of St. Francis of Assisi.

The church itself is less visited than the grotto below, but it is a lovely example of Crusader architecture.

Leaving St. Joseph's, turn left and return to the restrooms and walk through the gate and straight down to the entrance of the market.

7. THE MARKET

(*Souq* in Arabic, *Shuk* in Hebrew)

*9am to 5pm Mon, Tue, Thurs, Fri; 9am to 2pm Wed & Sat;
closed Sundays. Note: these hours are flexible*

Relatively small, the Nazareth market caters more to the locals than the tourists, which means it's a great place to look, haggle and soak in local atmosphere.

Walk straight into the market until you see a lane going left. Turn left here and walk a short distance. Where the lane ends, turn right. Walk a short distance until you notice two grayish columns on either side of an iron gate on your right – this is the Synagogue Church.

A shopkeeper keeps warm in his carpet shop.

8. GREEK-CATHOLIC SYNAGOGUE CHURCH

9am to 12:30pm & 2:30-6pm Mon, Tue, Thur & Fri; 9:30am to 12:30pm Wed & Sat; closed Sundays. Small donation, please.

The Greek Catholic Synagogue Church is used by the local Arab Christian community. The site of Jesus' synagogue is to its left.

Before going into the church, go a little further left and enter the room with the synagogue sign above.

Walk down the steps to a Crusader or medieval room, built on the traditional site of the synagogue where Jesus would have learned to read. However, Scripture has a less sympathetic story to tell about the reception Jesus gets in his hometown.

He went to Nazareth, where he had been brought up, and on the Sabbath day he went into the synagogue, as was his custom. He stood up to read, and the scroll of the prophet Isaiah was handed to him. Unrolling it, he found the place where it is written:

> *"The Spirit of the Lord is on me, because he has anointed me to proclaim good news to the poor. He has sent me to proclaim freedom for the prisoners and recovery of sight for the blind, to set the oppressed free, to proclaim the year of the Lord's favor."*
>
> Luke 4:16-19

Melkites

The Melkite or Greek Catholic Church numbers more than a million worldwide. Though they follow the Eastern Orthodox Church service, they acknowledge the supremacy of the Pope. Melkite comes from the Syriac word for "king" or "emperor."

Because of the name of this site in the Middle Ages was Arabic, *Madrassat el-Meseeh* ("school of the Messiah"), is today believed to be Jesus' synagogue.

Though little is known about synagogues during the Second Temple period, we do know that people would assemble on the Sabbath to hear the scriptures read. Another function was instruction. Boys were taught to read Hebrew and pray either in the synagogue itself or a room adjacent to it.

In Byzantine times, Nazareth was still Jewish (and Judeo-Christian) and the synagogue was a big attraction for Christian pilgrims coming from all over the Roman Empire. One could assume that the site of the synagogue was in the collective memory of the Hebrew Christians here and this medieval vault is in the vicinity of that synagogue. (With Nazareth's small population in the first century, one can safely assume there was only one house of prayer.) Adjacent to the synagogue is the Greek Catholic Church. Entering the Greek Catholic Church, notice that there is an *ico-*

The present Greek-Catholic church next to the site of Jesus' synagogue

The site of the "Synagogue Church" where Jesus read from Isaiah.

nostasis separating the priest from the worshippers, as in an Orthodox church. The church, topped with a central dome between two towers, is reminiscent of eastern churches, but this is hard to see from the surrounding market.

Leaving the church, go back to the main market entrance.

OTHER SITES IN NAZARETH

THE WHITE MOSQUE

9am-9pm, closed 11am-1pm; closed Fridays for prayer; admission free.

Remember that Nazareth is predominantly Muslim. The White Mosque was built by the Fahoum family under the reign of the infamous Achmed el Jazzar (the "butcher") Pasha, the legendary governor of the Galilee at the end of the 18th century. Jazzar successfully repelled Napoleon at Acre (Akko) in 1799.[4] The minaret of the mosque is clearly visible in the Roberts engraving of Nazareth from 1837.

Beautifully simple, the mosque represents the harmony of the people of Nazareth who worship one God. Remember, Jesus (called "Issa" in Arabic) is highly regarded by Muslims and in the Koran is called "the most blameless of all the prophets." However, the Koran denies his divinity, negating the virgin birth and crucifixion.

THE INTERNATIONAL CENTER OF MARY OF NAZARETH

Hours by appointment: Mon-Fri: 9am-12noon; 2pm-5pm; closed Tues; Sat: 2pm-5pm. ☎ *04-646-1266; mobile: 052-447-6083*

Opened in March 2011, this audio-visual presentation shows the history of Mary in the Holy Land.

Situated in the main market of the Old City, this new center is a must, especially for Catholic pilgrims. Presentations in English, French and other languages.

THE HERODIAN TOMB / SISTERS OF NAZARETH CONVENT

Visits by appointment only ☎ *04-655-4304. On the side street opposite the main entrance of the Basilica of the Annunciation, past the Casa Nova Hostel.*

The Sisters of Nazareth run a school for deaf and blind children and a guesthouse for tourists. Underneath the compound is, according to the sisters, a 1st-century Jewish tomb from the time of

---

4   Jazzar, who successfully defended the city of Akko (Acre) against Napoleon in 1799, earned his nickname by slicing off body pieces of subjects that "upset him."

The White Mosque is a refreshing reminder of coexistence between Muslims and Christians in Nazareth

Jesus, complete with rolling stone to seal the cave. However, this tomb raises a major question. Why is the tomb so close to the "dwellings" uncovered in 2009? Jewish burial sites are never near dwellings. Still, it is worth a visit.

EL BABOUR MILL SPICE SHOP

Daily 9am–5pm, Annunciation St. opposite Muslim cemetery.

In the late 18th century, Nazareth prospered as a market town offering, among other things, spices and coffee. This shop, located in an old mill, lets you sample the many sights, smell and colors of a bygone age. Be sure to try the *Majhoul* dates, sunflower seeds, pistachio nuts and fragrant exotic teas.

THE EVANGELICAL BAPTIST CHURCH – NAZARETH

Visits arranged by prior arrangement; ☎04-657-4370.
Services Sunday 10:30am, English translation available

On the main road just around the corner from Mary's Well Square in the direction of Tiberias, the Baptist Church was built in 1926 and is sadly neglected by many Evangelical groups visiting the Holy Land. The local pastor, Rev. Faud Sakhnini will gladly show you around the grounds.

MENSA CHRISTI CHURCH

To get here, follow the orange dots of the Jesus Trail through the market. The Mensa Christi church will be on your left as you ascend a long set of stairs up the hill behind the market. The key to the gate is kept by a family who lives on the lane opposite the entrance in the second door to the right. They are very friendly. Just ask for the key. Be sure to leave a donation of a few shekels per person.

The church was built in 1860 and is under the care of the Franciscans. First mentioned in the 18th century, the citizens of Nazareth said that Jesus appeared to his disciples here and ate dinner with them using the large rock outcropping as a table (*Mensa Christi* means "Christ's table" in Latin). This tradition does not appear in scripture and perhaps confuses this site with the site of the last appearance of the resurrected Jesus on the Sea of Galilee (where the Primacy of Peter Church sits, next to the Church of the Multiplication of the Loaves and Fishes) from John 21.

Climbing up the stairs and keeping to the sky-blue railing as you leave Mensa Christi, you will eventually come up to a road with an imposing church on the opposite side. This is the Salesian Church of Jesus the Adolescent and the Don Bosco School for Boys.

The Mensa Christi Church in Nazareth. Just ask the neighbors for the key!

SALESIAN CHURCH OF JESUS THE ADOLESCENT

Open daily in the afternoon. Closed Sunday.

One of the most beautiful churches in Israel, the Gothic style church took more than 20 years to finish. Dating from 1926, it's well worth walking the 400+ steps from the market. If you're pressed for time, bus 13 from the city center or a taxi will get you here.

TREMOR HILL – THE CHAPEL OF THE FRIGHT

Daily 8am–5pm; closed Sunday; Paul VI Street opposite the Galilee Hotel next to St. Clare's Convent.

Today, Tremor Hill is a care center for the elderly, but this spot is identified with the place where, according to Luke 4, Mary trembles with fear as she looks at Jesus avoiding being thrown off a cliff by an angry mob after delivering a sermon in the local synagogue, but was miraculously saved "by passing through the midst of them..." (Luke 4:30).

The act of throwing someone off a cliff seems rather odd, but in Jewish 1st-century eyes this was an allusion to the sacrifice made by the High Priest in Jerusalem on Yom Kippur, the Jewish Day of Atonement. The day would end when a "scapegoat" would be thrown off a mountain (called Azazel) to atone for the people's sins. "Azazel" is another name for hell in modern Hebrew.

NAZARETH VILLAGE

Daily 9am–5pm; closed Sunday; ☎*04-645 6042; www.nazarethvillage.com; Admission: 50NIS per person for individuals, 37NIS in a group of 10+, 34NIS for seniors and university students, 22NIS for children 7-18, free for children under 7 years old.*

THE JESUS TRAIL

The Jesus Trail is a hiking route from Nazareth to Capernaum (see map below) created by David Landis and Maoz Inon that follows Jesus' ministry in the Galilee. For the hikers among you who wish to further acquaint themselves with the northern part of Israel, *Hiking the Jesus Trail and other Biblical Walks in the Galilee*, is one of the best books on hiking in Israel I've encountered. The Jesus Trail in Nazareth marks the route from the Basilica of the Annunciation through the market up to the Mensa Christi church, Salesian Church and continues on to Zippori, Cana and the Sea of Galilee. Check out **www.jesustrail.com** for more information.

Nazareth Village is located southwest of the town center. Going south on Paulus VI street, you will come to an intersection marked with signs to the French Hospital. Follow the signs to the YMCA. Nazareth Village is located on the YMCA premises.

Nazareth Village offers tours that recreate a small Jewish agricultural settlement from the 1st century CE. Highly recommended. Self-service restaurant and gift shop on premises.

MOUNT OF THE PRECIPICE

You can walk to the overlook quite easily by going down from the Basilica circle and taking the new bypass road toward the tunnels, turning right at sign and going up the hill (see map on p. 12). At the car park, go left and follow the paved trail until you get to the Three Faiths Lookout.

Perhaps one of the best views in Israel, the whole Bible unfolds before you. To the north, the view is dominated by Mt. Tabor, the traditional site of the Transfiguration. Below is the Jezreel Valley in all its glory. Here Barak[5] and the prophetess Deborah[6] swooped down on the Canaanite forces below (Judges 4:1-16), and their general Sisera fled all the way to the Kishon River, only to get a stake through his temple in Jael's tent (Judges 4:17-21). Below is where King Saul consulted the medium of En Dor and learned of his fate the next day (1st Samuel 28: 5-25). This is also where Gideon and his commando force of 300 defeated the Midianites (Judges 6:9-22).

Today, we can see the Arab village of Iksal directly below us. The Jewish farm villages of Tel Adashim and Kfar Gidona tend their fertile fields. Across from them to the right is Kibbutz Mizra,

---

5   Barak ben Abinoam was an Israelite general from the tribe of Naphtali.

6   Deborah ("bee" in Hebrew) from the tribe of Ephraim, the wife of Lappidoth, was leading Israel at the time.

which, oddly enough, makes most of its income from the largest pork packing facility in the Middle East.

Opposite is the Hill of Moreh, with the town of Afula to its right; the village of Nain (see p. 103) is to the bottom left. In the distance are the mountains of Gilboa, cursed by David to be without rain. The mountains of the Gilead in present-day Jordan peep out on the horizon.

WHERE TO STAY

HOTELS

Rimonin Hotel
(☎04-550-0000; Paulus VI St.; www.rimonin.com)
Centrally located near Mary's Well on Paulus VI Street, and close to all the sites. Rooms run between $125-$150 per night with breakfast. Air conditioning, Internet and cable.

Golden Crown Nazareth Hotel
(☎04-650-8000; Mt. Precipice, Nazareth; www.goldencrown.co.il)
A hotel with 243 rooms which tends to cater to larger bus groups. Hotel is not well-located, but with great views and friendly staff.

St. Gabriel Hotel
(☎04-657-2133; 2 Salesian St.; www.stgabrielhotel.com/eng)
Best known for its views, somewhat difficult to find. Was a former convent. A double room with breakfast costs $120.

Rosary Sisters
(☎04-6554435; www.rsisters.com)
Simple no-frills accommodations with the Rosary Sister nuns.

HOSTELS

A refreshing alternative to hotels and usually cheaper, hostels are located in the old city of Nazareth, close to most of the sites. Rubbing shoulders with the locals is a great experience as the people of Nazareth are very friendly to visitors.

Fauzi Azar Inn

(☎04-602-0469, Old City Nazareth, www.fauziazarinn.com)
Situated in a former wealthy merchant's villa, this is my choice. Located in the heart of the old city, close to most of the sites in the tour. Run by entrepreneur Maoz Inon and the local Azar family, the Fauzi Azar Inn offers large, multi-bed rooms for hikers and backpackers as well as individual and family-sized rooms. Includes great breakfast and free Internet. Newly added deluxe rooms from $100 to $140 per night for a double including breakfast.

WHERE TO EAT

Nazareth is one of the best places to go off your diet! Falafel, hummus, shwarma (roasted turkey, like Greek *gyros*) and those great Arab cakes and cookies with black coffee or tea all are literally around every corner. For those with a more sophisticated palate (and willing to spend a little extra for an excellent meal), there are also some great sit-down restaurants.

Shwarma

Opposite the Mahroum Bakery on the other side of Paul the VI Street are a number of small restaurants with great shwarma. Falafel is also available. Falafel costs 15NIS (about $4); shwarma 20NIS.

El Sheich Restaurant

(☎04-656 7664; Rotary of Iksal Street off Paul VI St. opposite the Basilica. 8am to 5pm daily, closed Sunday)
Maybe the best hummus outside of Acre. Served with warm chick peas or fava beans on top with fresh pita bread, tomato and onion

on the side—it just doesn't get better than this. At about $5.00 per person, a must! Their falafel and shwarma are pretty good, too.

Diana
(☎04-657 2919; 51 Paul VI Street)
Still the favorite among Israelis, this is one of the best restaurants in the city. Lots of great food. Try the lamb kebabs with pine nuts. Everything is good. About $40 per meal. Closed Mondays.

Tishreen
(☎04-608-4666; 56 Al Bishara St.)
Located a stone's throw from Mary's Well Square, Tishreen (Arabic for October) boasts an original menu, it's no wonder that it's packed Thursday and Friday night with the folks from as far away as Tel Aviv. From $10-20 per meal.

Al-Reda
(☎04-608-4404; 23 Al Bishara St.)
Giving Diana stiff competition, Al-Reda has a great atmosphere with not only Middle Eastern cuisine but also French and Italian food. The floor above is a guesthouse that overlooks the Basilica of the Annunciation. Closed Mondays. From $15-30/meal.

Mahroum Sweets
Don't go where the tourists stop, the real Mahroum Bakery is just opposite El Sheich. Go for a cheese-filled sweet delicacy called *knaffe*. They won't have it until after 11am, but it is well worth the wait. At 10NIS for a large piece your money is well spent!

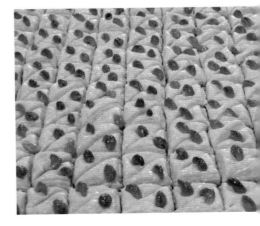

Baklauwa (baklava) cakes at Mahroum Bakery. Yum!

This is the Roman *decumanus*. Note that the streets are paved in local stone (in this case, limestone). Dated from the 2nd - 3rd century, they were in use until the Arab conquest in 637 CE.

Zippori

Capital of the Galilee

Zippori National Park

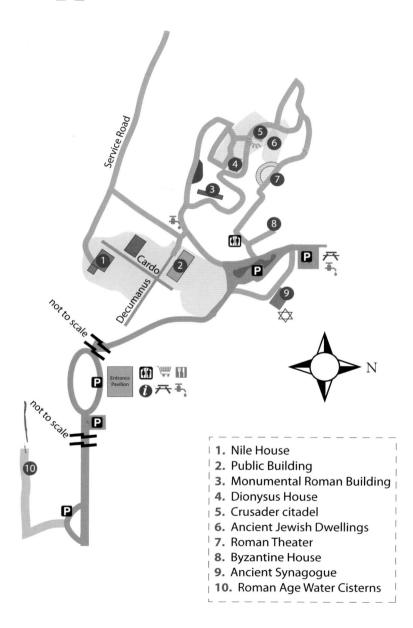

1. Nile House
2. Public Building
3. Monumental Roman Building
4. Dionysus House
5. Crusader citadel
6. Ancient Jewish Dwellings
7. Roman Theater
8. Byzantine House
9. Ancient Synagogue
10. Roman Age Water Cisterns

TOUR 2 SNAPSHOT

Length of Tour
Allow two hours for the national park, up to five hours if you plan to visit the moshav.

Hours
April–September: 8am–5pm; October–March: 8am–4pm
Last entry one hour before closing.
☎ 04-656-8272

Entrance Fee
27NIS adult; 14NIS children 5 to 18 (See N.P Entry Cards, p. 188)

How to Get There
By bus, from Nazareth take bus 28, 28A or 343 and get off at Zippori Junction. From Nazareth Illit or Haifa, take bus 342. Walk to the brown information sign and follow the 3 km long road to the park entrance.

By car, from Nazareth take Route 79 west; from Tiberias take Route 77 west to Hamovil Junction and turn left to Route 79 east.

TOUR 2 INTRODUCTION

The second tour begins at the entrance to the moshav (small collective farm) of Zippori and Zippori National Park. This is on Route 79 between Nazareth and Ha-Movil Junction.

Why does the National Park of Zippori figure so prominently in this book?

Zippori (Sephoris in Greek) was the largest urban center situated on the main road between the coast and the province of Syria. It was and still is surrounded by rich and fertile soil and situated on high ground, its strategic value was unquestionable.

The truly remarkable collection of mosaics on the site from the 3rd to 6th century CE, the well-preserved Roman streets and boasting one of the best preserved synagogue floors in Israel, all make this site highly recommended.

We know nothing about "the missing years," between the time Jesus "went missing" when he was 12 years old (Luke 2:41-49) and then was found teaching the sages near the Sanhedrin (the Jewish high council of learning, sort of a 72-man Supreme Court) until his baptism by his second cousin, John, in the Jordan River (Matthew 3:13-17, Mark 1:9-11, Luke 3:21-22 , John 1:29-34).

Yeshua

Jesus' name in Hebrew was Yeshua (Joshua in English) which translates as "redeemer."

What was Jesus doing? Where did he go?

The truth is not known. Most scholars think he stayed close to home, or at least in Galilee and, with his father, worked as a builder. Tradition has Joseph dying when Jesus had reached maturity and he may have taken on full family responsibilities, at least until one or more of his "brothers" was old enough to take his place as the main family breadwinner.

Some think he did other things.

The English poet William Blake wrote a poem called Jerusalem in which Jesus wanders in the company of Joseph of Arimithea, as far north as the Roman province of Britannica:

> And did those feet in ancient time Walk
> upon England's mountains green?
> And was the holy Lamb of God
> On England's pleasant pastures seen?

I'm rather hesitant to agree with Blake that Jesus made it to Britain; on the other hand, I don't think that he stayed "on the farm" in Nazareth until he was baptized by John.

There is good reason to believe that Jesus and Joseph made their living as builders, and quite near them was the boom town of the Galilee, Zippori. Jesus and Joseph may have quite logically worked in construction of this Roman-style city.

ZIPPORI NATIONAL PARK

Zippori was probably re-founded in the 2nd Century BCE, when Jewish King John Hycanus "judaized" the Galilee. (It was originally founded 600 years before and destroyed by the Assyrian Empire in the 8th century BCE.)

The city had a strong wall that withstood Egyptian King Ptolemy VIII around 100 BCE. When the kingdom of Israel was conquered by Roman general Pompey in 63 BCE, Zippori was made into the governing city of the Galilee.

Name Origins

The Babylonian Talmud states that Zippori got its name because it sits on a mountain like a bird (tzipor in Hebrew).

Zippori (Greek: Sepphoris) was destroyed in a civil disturbance at the time of the death of Herod the Great (4 BCE). Josephus tells us that Sepphoris was burnt to the ground in this so-called "Varus Revolt," yet archaeologists have found no evidence of this.

Zippori was certainly not a large town then, but it would later be the capital of the Galilee when Herod's son, Herod Antipas, inherited the Galilee in 4 BCE. Zippori was strategically positioned near the main road leading from the south, the *Via Maris*, and the east-west road from the port of Acre (Ptolemais) to Tiberias and then to Damascus. It was rebuilt and enlarged and it was probably then, and in the following years, that Joseph and Jesus found employment as builders in the city's reconstruction.

Situated some 4 km (as the bird flies) from Nazareth, it would have been an ideal work place for Joseph and his son, Jesus, to practice their professions in the building trade.

Zippori is not only an important city in Jewish Mishnaic history but also Crusader history. It is from Zippori that the crusading army under the weak-willed king Guy de Lusignan set off to meet their destiny at the Battle of the Horns of Hattin. Saladin defeated them on July 4th, 1187, bringing to an end the first Crusader Kingdom of Jerusalem. Only a small portion of the Holy Land was won back by King Richard the Lionheart four years later.

The Crusading army gathered at Zippori Springs, which is situated on the modern road into Zippori. Note the remains of a building covering the spring on your right as you enter the road 7926 off the main Route 79.

Plan to spend a good part of the day visiting the Zippori National Park. Most of the remains are from the Roman/Byzantine and Crusader era, and the wealth of mosaics, baths, theater, markets and public buildings makes Zippori worth your time.

Begin the visit by paying at the gate, 2.6 km (1.6 mi) from the spring. Walk another 800 m (about 2,600 ft) to the car park. On the opposite side is an ancient pool (1) (called the "Mashad" Pool, after the springs which fed it) that may have served as a swimming pool in Roman times. An aqueduct brought water here from the neighboring hills to the east. More about that aqueduct later (see p. 76).

The nearby visitors center has a gift shop, restrooms and a model of the site. Though outdated, it gives the visitor a good idea of the scope of the historic city. Don't miss the short film shown in a small room next to the gift shop.

Leave the visitors' center and walk down to the excavated road (3). Walk down the staircase slightly to the left.

As you walk these ancient streets, on the right and left were sidewalks which would have been paved with mosaics under a portico of terracotta roofs. These sidewalks led to shops that sold produce and other necessities such as clothes, pottery, household goods etc. The farmers of the Galilee not only came to town to sell their produce, but also to buy necessities.

URBAN PLANNING

The Romans were the first civilization to have urban planning. Romans carefully paved north-south streets (cardo; pl. cardi) and east-west streets (decumanus; pl. decumani) to make an easily navigable grid, a concept still used in modern city planning.

Josephus said Zippori was the largest city in the Galilee[1] when the future emperor Vespasian accepted the surrender of the city in 68 CE, almost 40 years after Jesus' death. So it is safe to deduce that if the city was destroyed in the Varus Revolt in 4 BCE and 72 years later was the biggest city in Galilee, a lot of building must have been going on in those years. If we are to assume that Joseph and Jesus were indeed *tektonoi* (builders), there is a very good chance that they worked a lot there.

Christian scholar Dr. Paul Wright of Jerusalem University College suggests that Joseph and Jesus trekked from Nazareth to Zippori on Sundays, worked and slept over during and week and came home Fridays before the Sabbath.[2]

This theory is attractive, not only because it makes a lot of sense, but because here Jesus would have been exposed to the sages that resided in Zippori who were renowned for their wisdom. More importantly, he would have had a chance to learn with them and from their books and libraries—a rare thing in rural Nazareth.

As you reach the "crossroads" between the decamanus and the cardo, look down at the paving stones.

---

1   Josephus' *The Jewish War*, Book 3:34
2   From Paul Wright's book *Greatness, Grace and Glory*, Carta, 2007

There are games etched onto the stones by the inhabitants of Zippori in the 3rd-5th century CE. You can imagine the children playing games on the road while their parents were carrying on their business in the nearby shops.

Stop at the crossroad. Looking down any street, you will notice ruts made more than 1,500 years ago by wagons carrying harvests from the outlying villages to the markets here. (This is quite visible in the photo on p. 55).

The grid system here of north-south streets bisected by east-west streets is the hallmark of Roman urban planning. This part of the city is post-Jesus, but well worth a visit.

Walking to the end of the street, you come to a modern structure covering the "Nile House."

1. NILE HOUSE

Archaeologists aren't exactly sure of the purpose of this magnificent structure, but most agree it may have housed one of the many markets the Talmud says were here in the 3rd to 5th centuries CE.

Games more than 1,500 years old are etched onto the paving stones.

The building had three major halls connected with corridors. Of note is the Amazon mosaic. Notice that the Amazons have both their breasts when, according to legend, Amazons would cut off their right breast in order to draw their bow more easily.

As you walk through the rooms, the geometric patterns of these mosaics are truly dizzying.

You will come to the largest mosaic, aptly called the Nile Mosaic because of the river bisecting the mosaic from left to right. The famous lighthouse of Alexandria is on your left, with fire lighting its beacon. Notice how the ancients believed that the source of the Nile was a giant hippopotamus spewing water out of its mouth.

A hunting scene adorns the bottom part of the mosaic. Notice the cats chasing mice on the lower left. The artist whimsically has a mouse run half off the mosaic - with only its backside visible!

Amazons on the hunt. Tally-ho!

ORPHEUS

According to Greek mythology, Orpheus was the greatest musician who ever lived. He tried to rescue his wife, Eurydice, from Hades. The god of the underworld made only one condition. He could not look back until he had reached sunlight. As he reached daylight, he turned around to see if his wife was behind him, only to lose her forever. If this story sounds familiar, you may notice similarities to the story of Lot's wife turning to a pillar of salt as she looked back on Sodom and Gemorrah (Genesis 19).

Return to the Cardo and continue walking until you come to a wooden staircase on your left. Standing on top, you are looking at the famous Orpheus Mosaic.

Notice Orpheus playing the lyre. Animals are above him and on the ground at his feet, listening attentively.

This mosaic was originally on the floor of a villa. It decorated the triclinium, or main entertainment room. In Roman times, families would have the main meal in the evening, and entertaining guests was the order of the day.

Couches were placed in an open square shape, and the guests would recline (taken from the word *triclinium*) and not only enjoy the meal, but between courses, would hear poetry read, or enjoy dancers, acrobats, and other entertainment. The status of the host would often depend on how lavish these meals were and how well-decorated the triclinium was.

The lower part of the mosaic in front depicts some scenes from this lost world of Byzantine feasts (see photo on next page).

The center frame shows the guests around a semi-circular open table enjoying what seems to be some sort of bird. This type of seating arrangement was a later development in the Roman/Byzantine world in contrast to the more formal seating arrangement which you will see later in the tour.

To the right are two guests playing a board game and, to the left, two men who are either dancers or wrestlers are entertaining the diners.

The wall that cuts through this mosaic is the apse of a church that was built over the *triclinium*. The building was approximately 18 m (60 ft) long, built in the 4th or 5th century in the typical *basilica* style with a central nave, two side aisles and an apse, visible down on the right, where Mass was celebrated.

Return to the Cardo and go up the stairs to the left and walk towards the hill. Notice that you are walking parallel to the decumanus on your left. To the right, notice the mosaic floors of the building which is our next stop. With the water cooler on your left, turn right and go to the wooden observation platform.

Late Byzantine dinner party

2. THE PUBLIC BUILDING

Calling this structure "the Public Building" is the archaeologists' way of saying "I really don't know what this was." Because the Talmud speaks of 18,000 markets in Zippori, a good guess is that it held a market, whose floors were decorated with various mosaics. Situated on a main road between the Mediterranean Sea and Damascus, and right in the agricultural heartland of the Galilee, Zippori was an ideal place for farmers to bring their crops to market to sell to the merchants who lived here.

Looking at the floor below, notice the quaint mosaic of a duck astride a lotus flower to the left. It is shaded by the two walls that project out. They are covered with a fresco that dates to Roman times.

This would be a good time to refill your water bottles, so walk back to the water cooler we passed earlier and when you've refreshed yourself walk to the remains of the building slightly to your left.

3. THE MONUMENTAL ROMAN BUILDING

Centrally located between the acropolis or upper city and the lower city, this building may have housed the city's library and/or archive. Niches found in the western wall suggest this use.

Libraries are of particular interest. Did Jesus, when he finished a day's work at Zippori, go the to town library to read, learn and converse with city's learned men?

Return to the direction of the water cooler and turn left at the path which goes up the hill. Climb up the stairs which are surrounded by prickly pear cactus. At the top of the stairs, turn right and follow the trail until you reach the "Dionysus House."

4. THE DIONYSUS HOUSE

The "Dionysus House" or "Roman Villa" is a building dated to the early 3rd century CE. This was a private dwelling probably owned by an extremely wealthy individual. Why wealthy? Built in the better part of town (where it could catch the cool evening breezes in this warm climate), its sheer size and the marvelous mosaic that decorates the triclinium identify this structure as extraordinary.

Wait a moment or two and let your eyes acclimate themselves to the dim light. In front of you are artists' representations of the villa itself (to your left) and the triclinium in use. This triclinium predates the Orpheus mosaic by a century or two. (Most scholars date the Dionysus Mosaic from the end of the 3rd century CE, while the Orpheus mosaic was laid in the 5th century). The guests are sitting in what appears to be an open square, reclining on couches. To your right is a covered opening showing a water cistern, and photographs depicting the excavation and unique

The "Mona Lisa of the Galilee"

preservation carried out by the Israel Antiquities Authority on this remarkable floor.

In the Orpheus mosaic the guests are sitting around a semi-circular table, which seems to give a more democratic feeling to the meal. Perhaps the onset of Christianity gave the guests and hosts alike a feeling of kinship and unity.

Going up the stairs, the entire mosaic comes into view. Aptly called the Dionysus Mosaic, the mosaic depicts 15 scenes in the life of Dionysus, the god who brought the gift of wine to man. Captioned in Greek, the T-shaped mosaic shows the Greco-Roman influence on the region of Israel, and more specifically, the Jewish population residing here.

Measuring 9x7 m (29.5x23 ft), the mosaic covers the floor like a carpet. The 15 center panels depict the god Dionysus and his doings (a drinking contest with Hercules, his wedding to Ariadne, etc). An outer frame consisting of twenty-two "medallions" depicts hunters and their prey. What dominates the onlooker is the beautiful woman, known as the "Mona Lisa of the Galilee."

This portrait may be Israel's greatest art treasure. The workmanship is truly remarkable. From the sheen of her cheek, to the delicate pomegranate earrings, this is a masterpiece.

The question is, who could afford such work? If this does, indeed, date from the beginning of the 3rd century, are we in the house of the illustrious Rabbi Judah Ha-Nasi (Judah the prince or president)? The most famous of Zippori's residents, he lived here until his death circa 215 CE, redacting the Mishna (the six-volume work codifying the oral commentaries on the Torah). The rabbi was well-connected, supposedly even on first name terms with emperor Caricalla. He also was purported to be one of the wealthiest citizens of the Roman province of Palestina Secunda. Are we in his house? He was supposed to have promoted the Greek language (while speaking Hebrew at home). But what about the pagan imagery of the mosaic? Was it just "art for art's sake?" We may never know the answer.

The far end of the mosaic shows a Nile scene with hunters killing a crocodile. (The artist probably never saw one in the flesh—notice the long ears!). This is a later addition to the mosaic, probably a repair job. Notice how this latter artist's work falls short of the original.

The Parks Authority does a nice job of explaining the mosaic with informative signs all around the platform, but before leaving, go down to the Mona Lisa again. Turning left, you come to a 1,800 year old indoor privy. The Mosaic says ΗΓΙΑ (Greek: *hegia* means "health", note connection to English word "hygiene"). Waste was sluiced out by pouring water down the opening. This demonstrates the sophisticated sewage network so prevalent in Roman cities in the 3rd century.

When finished reading and taking photos, exit up the stairs.

As you leave the villa, turn right. In front of you is a large square building made of local limestone. That's our next stop.

5. THE CRUSADER CITADEL

Built at the same time as the nearby Crusader church here, this castrum[3] style structure served as an observation fort and citadel. It is constructed from stones of different periods, the most interesting of which are the Roman sarcophagi in the corners of the fort. The holes in these limestone coffins were made by grave robbers about 700 years before the Crusader era.

---

3   *Castrum* is Latin for a fortified position surrounded by a wall.

When the first Crusader Kingdom fell at the Battle of Horns of Hattin, the Crusader army set out to meet their doom from Zippori. The army assembled under their foolish king, Guy de Lusignan. This fort was then in the possession of the Knights Templar who, with the Knights Hospital, urged the impressionable Guy to fight Saladin on one of the hottest days of the year in an area with no water.

The entrance is not Crusader. The fort lay in ruins after the Crusader's final defeat in 1291. The Bedouin ruler of the Galilee, Dahar el-Omar in the late 18th century, rebuilt the site and turned it into a school for the Arab inhabitants who later settled here.

Climbing to the observation roof, you can see why this place was important strategically. On a clear day, you can see Mt. Hermon in the north, the city of Haifa to the west, Nazareth to the south and all around the fruitful plains of the Turan and Netofa valleys.

The Crusader Citadel

But the question is, in all of this magnificent archaeological park, where did Jesus and Joseph work? Look below you to the west. The remains just under the citadel are of the oldest quarter in Zippori. Were some of these homes built by Jesus?

As you leave the Citadel, turn right and walk to the "Jewish Quarter."

6. ANCIENT JEWISH DWELLINGS

Ritual Purity

The things that made you impure and thus in need of a dip in a mikvah were any type of bodily discharge, any type of inflammation of the skin or, the most defiling, any contact with a dead body.

I call this the "Jewish Quarter" because of the number of Jewish ritual baths (*mikva'ot*) found here. Jews living at the time of Jesus had to make a pilgrimage to Jerusalem three times a year. In order to make the pilgrimage, one had to ensure ritual purity.

In front of you may well be the remains of homes built by Joseph and Jesus.

Zippori's "Jewish Quarter" viewed from the Citadel

Zippori's Roman theater with a view to the Beit Netofa Valley.

Walk to the blue information sign. The building below with the red terracotta shingles is the convent of St. Anne and a girls' school. Turn right and follow the path to the Roman theater.

7. THE ROMAN THEATER

Not much remains of Zippori's Roman theater. Built at the end of the 1st century or the beginning of the 2nd century CE, it held 4,500 spectators. Most of the masonry from the structure was used in secondary buildings by the Crusaders and later the Arabs.

Just a note on what was shown on stage: Roman citizens liked to watch light comedies, acrobats, clowns, poetry readings and popular renditions of mythological stories. (The word myth in Greek originally meant "truth").

Performances were held during the day, never at night, and admission was free. The bill was footed usually by a local politician who wanted to curry favor with the citizens.

Follow the exit sign and walk to the modern buildings. Inside are restrooms. Walk down the first set of stairs and turn left to the "Byzantine House."

8. THE BYZANTINE HOUSE

Not a large building, but a quaint mosaic floor. The artist made rows of crosses, rosettes and pomegranates and birds with red collars on the top. The "carpet" is bordered with a braid design.

Return to the staircase and descend to the parking lot. Cross the lot and on the right is another staircase to the ancient synagogue.

9. THE ANCIENT SYNAGOGUE

Built almost 400 years after Christ, this synagogue was one of many in Zippori. Discovered by accident in 1993, the floor is best viewed from the raised platform to the right upon entering. Walk around the mosaic and start to view it on this platform near the entrance. Excellent signs explain the seven sections of the work.

The late Ehud Netzer and Zeev Weis, the two main archaeologists who have excavated Zippori for the Hebrew University of Jerusalem, named the mosaic "Promise and Redemption." The promise begins with the first scene below us, where Abraham entertains the three angels who have come to Mamre to announce that Sarai (later Sarah), though "stricken in years," is to have a child (Gen 18:10). Though very little remains of this panel, it is reconstructed to show how it probably looked.

The next panel shows the binding of Isaac on the right, and Abraham's two servants waiting at the foot of Mt. Moriah (regarded as the Temple Mount in Jerualem, under the present-day Dome of the Rock).

However, aside from the usual Jewish motifs of menorahs and utensils from the Second Temple, two things stand out: the use of Greek in the floor of the synagogue and a pagan symbol of the zodiac as the centerpiece of the building.

Aramaic, not Greek, was the mother tongue of the Jews in Galilee at that time. Were there perhaps businessmen from Alexandria (where the native tongue of Jews was Greek) residing at Zippori?

Signs of the Zodiac on the Floor of the synagogue at Zippori. Astrology or early Kabala (Jewish Mysticism)? "Kabala," which means "receiving," refers to the mystical interpretations of the Hebrew Bible.

Astrology was not accepted by mainstream rabbis in the Talmudic period. However, the sages mention the Jewish community of Zippori as not being too terribly observant of Jewish law. Perhaps this "backsliding," showing pagan imagery in a holy building, illustrates this.

One last thing: notice the flames on the menorah candelabra. Their flames all bend in the same direction. The prevailing winds are from the northeast— exactly as depicted on the mosaic!

Leave the synagogue and walk back to the visitors center. After a rest stop and a visit to the small shop, return to the gate (and park your car there if you've got one). To the right of the gate and ticket office is a path that leads to the water cisterns.

10. THE ROMAN AGE WATER CISTERNS

The Romans were magnificent engineers. Bringing water from outlying areas into urban centers was one of their specialties. Before us is a reservoir dug into the already "cracked" limestone.

More than 850 ft long (260 m) and holding 4,300 m^3 of water (more than 1 million gallons!), it could have supplied the city with enough water for 15,000 residents in comfort for a year.

Two sets of aqueducts brought water from the nearby springs in the nearby Nazareth mountains. Walking through them, you'll notice they excavated the cisterns a little too close to the surface, hence the collapsed roofs.

Part of the water system at Zippori.

ST. ANNE'S CRUSADER CHURCH

Leave the park and return to the main road into Zippori. Turn right and enter the moshav. If the gate is closed, wait a minute or two until a resident opens it to enter. Take the main road about 1.5 kms until you reach the sign marking St. Anne's Church. The sign is in Italian and hard to see. It will be on your right. Opposite the car park is a grey metal door. Go through it and walk down the stone steps. Take the path to the left and walk down around the building. The entrance is to the right.

One oral tradition tells that the Virgin Mary was from Zippori, though most Christian scholars would say that Jerusalem holds this honor. (The St. Anne's Crusader Church just inside St. Stephan's Gate at the Bethesda Pools celebrates this spot.)

St. Anne's Crusader Church, Zippori

A lesser-known tradition has Joanna born here, too.

Joanna the wife of Chuza, the manager of Herod's household; Susanna; and many others. These women were helping to support them out of their own means. Luke 8:3

Crusader Zippori (*Le Sephorie*) was perhaps in need of a pedigree of some sort and after 1187 CE Jerusalem was no longer in European hands. Perhaps transferring Mary's birthplace to Zippori made Frankish lands seem a little bit more important.

WHERE TO STAY

While most will opt to stay in the immediate area of Nazareth for this trip, you can spend a very pleasant evening on a working farm that doubles as a bed and breakfast.

Zippori Country Cottages
(☎04-646-2647, 057-782-9568; Moshav Zippori, www.zipori.com) Comprised of six log cabins, each of which can easily sleep a family. Managed by former North Americans Suzy and Mitch Pilcer, this can be a great way to enjoy the Galilee's scenery and atmosphere. $120 per night for a couple with breakfast. Add another $25 per child. Slightly higher on weekends and Jewish holidays.

WHERE TO EAT

There are actually two great finds at Zippori for food and lodging. Zippori Country Cabins provide a country breakfast with accommodations, but if you want a truly Galilean lunch or dinner, I warmly recommend *Tzon-El Dairy.*

Owner Jeffrey Ellis runs a goat farm and produces some of the best gourmet cheeses in the country. Meals must be pre-arranged. Ellis Farm (☎04-646-9536; Moshav Zippori; http://tzonel.com).

Mt. Tabor in the Jezreel Valley, with the villages of Deburiya and Umm el Ghanim to the right and left, and the village of Iksal in the foreground.

Cana, Mt. Tabor, and Nain

The Real and Imagined Sites near Nazareth

Around Nazareth, Cana, Mt. Tabor, Nain

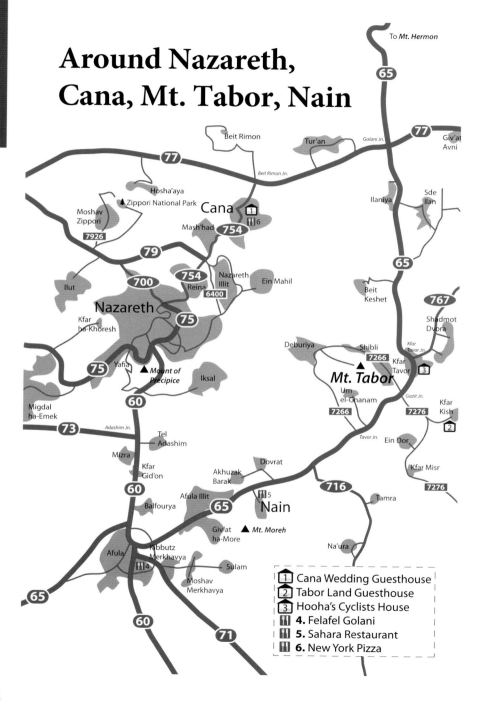

To *Mt. Hermon*

65

77

Giv'at Avni

Tur'an

Golani Jn.

Beit Rimon

77

Beit Rimon Jn.

Hosha'aya

▲ Zippori National Park

Ilaniya

Sde Ilan

Moshav Zippori

7926

Mash'had

Cana 1 6

754

65

79

754

Nazareth Illit

Ein Mahil

Beit Keshet

767

Ilut

700

Reina

6400

Shadmot Dvora

Nazareth

75

Kfar Tavor Jn.

Kfar ha-Khoresh

Deburiya

Shibli

Kfar Tavor

7266

3

75

Yafia

▲ *Mount of Precipice*

Iksal

Mt. Tabor

Um el-Ghanam

Gazit Jn.

Kfar Kish

Migdal ha-Emek

60

7266

7276

2

73

Adashim Jn.

Tel Adashim

Tavor Jn.

Ein Dor

Mizra

Kfar Gid'on

Dovrat

Kfar Misr

Akhuzak Barak

60

Afula Illit

65

5

Nain

716

7276

Tamra

Balfourya

Giv'at ha-More

▲ *Mt. Moreh*

Na'ura

Afula

Kibbutz Merkhavya

4

Sulam

65

Moshav Merkhavya

60

71

1	Cana Wedding Guesthouse
2	Tabor Land Guesthouse
3	Hooha's Cyclists House
🍴	**4.** Felafel Golani
🍴	**5.** Sahara Restaurant
🍴	**6.** New York Pizza

TOUR 3 SNAPSHOT

Sites

Begin in Kfar Cana at the Catholic Wedding Church. Continue to Mount Tabor to enjoy the view and the Franciscan church. Finish your day in Nain with a visit to the church associated with the healing of the widow's son. Bear in mind that the main church in Cana is closed between noon and 2pm, and the church on Mount Tabor is closed on Saturdays.

Length

Half day

Type of Tour

Driving, also possible by public transport (see each site page for transport details)

TOUR 3 INTRODUCTION

After Jesus was baptized by his kinsman John in the Jordan River, his ministry began. The book of John tells us that his first miracle took place at a wedding in the nearby Galilean village of Cana.

In the company of Peter, John and James, Jesus ascended a mountain and appeared along with Moses and Elijah in a shining, transformed state.

Later, Jesus raised the widow's son from the dead in Nain.

Here in the Galilee, Jesus met God the Father, performed miracles and taught through his unique parables. Let us now go on a journey to these places to learn about the deeds of this remarkable man.

CANA

On the third day a wedding took place at Cana in Galilee. Jesus' mother was there, and Jesus and his disciples had also been invited to the wedding. When the wine was gone, Jesus' mother said to him, "They have no more wine." "Woman, why do you involve me?" Jesus replied. "My hour has not yet come." His mother said to the servants, "Do whatever he tells you." Nearby stood six stone water jars, the kind used by the Jews for ceremonial washing, each holding from twenty to thirty gallons. Jesus said to the servants, "Fill the jars with water"; so they filled them to the brim. Then he told them, "Now draw some out and take it to the master of the banquet."

They did so, and the master of the banquet tasted the water that had been turned into wine. He did not realize where it had come from, though the servants who had drawn the water knew. Then he called the bridegroom aside and said, "Everyone brings out

Visiting Cana (Kfar Cana)

Hours
Wedding Church (Franciscan) open Mon-Sat; 8am-12pm, 2-6pm (summer) and 2-5pm (winter). Greek Orthodox Church open daily 8-5 by appointment.

How to Get There
By bus, catch bus 431, 28, 28A, or 30. north from Mary's Well. Sheruts also depart from Mary's Well in Nazareth to Cana every 15-20 min. for 7NIS per person. Journey of about 20 min.

By car, take Route 75 south at Beit Rimon Junction if coming either from Haifa or Tiberias; if you are driving from Nazareth, take the main road (Pope John VI Street) and go straight all the way north (on Route 75) until the town of Kfar Cana.

the choice wine first and then the cheaper wine after the guests have had too much to drink; but you have saved the best till now."

What Jesus did here in Cana of Galilee was the first of the signs through which he revealed his glory; and his disciples believed in him.

John 2:1-11

Cana is also mentioned as the hometown of the disciple Nathanael and where Jesus healed the nobleman's son (John 4:46-54).

According to John, Jesus' first two miracles happen in Cana. It must have been a pretty important place.

It is worth noting that all the references to Cana appear in the Gospel of John; Matthew, Mark and Luke don't mention the town.

85

WHERE IS THE "REAL" CANA?

The present-day town of Kafr Cana is 8 km (less than 5 mi) northwest of Nazareth. It is traditionally identified as "Cana of the Galilee" where Jesus performed his first miracle of turning of water into wine.

Kafr Cana boasts four churches: two Catholic, one Greek Orthodox and one Greek-Catholic (Melkite).

The abundance of functioning churches and the remains of a synagogue, a Byzantine church and a Crusader church over the Catholic church seems to vindicate the adage "holy places stay holy."

However, some Christian scholars point to the ruins of an ancient Jewish village in the nearby Netofa Valley more than 20 km away from Nazareth, Khirbet Kana, as the true biblical Cana.

Khirbet Kana is a few kilometers east of the Arab village of Kafr Manda and a few kilometers southeast of the Second Temple period town of Jopata (Yodfat), the place where the first-century Jewish historian (and infamous traitor) Flavius Josephus connived to be captured by the Romans led by General (and future emperor) Vespasian.

Khirbet Kana contains the remains of a small Jewish village (mainly some water cisterns; the rest of the town was totally destroyed by the Romans) and the ruins of a synagogue or church.

KAFR CANA OR KHIRBET KANA?
WHERE IS CANA OF GALILEE?

Excavated in the late 1990s and into the present decade, an underground Crusader chapel was found at Khirbet Kana.

In his excellent book, *In the Steps of Jesus*, Peter Walker argues that the deserted ruins of Khirbet Kana are the real deal. He bases this on its location in relation to Capernaum and how much time it would take to walk from there to the now-destroyed town. Dr. Paul Wright in his book *Greatness, Grace and Glory* also prefers the ruins to the Greek and Catholic shrines of Cana.

Walker writes that the nobleman's son recovered at 1 o'clock in the afternoon the previous day. He met messengers half-way between Capernaum and Khirbet Kana. Kafr Cana is just too close by his reckoning. Khirbet Kana, 8 mi (13 km) away, fits the narrative better because it is far enough to be halfway between the towns.

The question is: Why would the Crusaders built a large church in today's Kafr Cana and also erect a chapel celebrating the same event more than 10 km away?

The Crusaders usually built religious edifices on older, Byzantine sites. They built a huge church in Kafr Cana, but a small, underground chapel at Khirbet Cana. Perhaps they, like us today, knew of both sites and wanted to honor both. Then, like now, most pilgrims visited Kafr Cana, the site closer to Nazareth. Perhaps it is best to remember the biblical events and not to worry so much about exactly where they happened geographically.

I do not include a side trip to Khirbet Kana in this book. For those who would like to go for a visit, it's a short walk either from Kafr Manda or Yodfat.[1] For a place of silent contemplation, there are many more accessible places.

Let's get back to the Cana event, the first miracle, when Jesus turned water into wine.

---

1   The excellent hikers' guide to the Jesus Trail discusses this in detail (p. 191).

MOTHER IS ALWAYS RIGHT

When reading Scripture, we often forget that every word is important. Look at the third word in John 2:1— "third." "On the **third** day there was a wedding in Cana of Galilee..."

In the Jewish calendar, the third day is Tuesday. Tuesday is a particularly auspicious day to marry in Judaism. I was married on a Tuesday, too. Why does it seem to be a good day to get married?

In the book of Genesis, the Almighty created land and seas "and God saw that it was good" (Gen 1:10), and also created grasses, trees and fruit and again "God saw that it was good" (Gen 1:12).

This is the only instance in the story of creation that God said "and it was good" twice the same day. That is why in the past and up to the present day, Jews will try to do anything of meaning on a Tuesday: weddings, important events (like sending a book to a publisher!), and just about anything of real importance.

We also learn in John 2 that Jesus already has disciples and both Jesus, his mother and the disciples are invited to a wedding in the nearby town of Cana.

So this must have been a wedding of one of Mary's kinsman. I say this on the assumption that when the wine runs out, Mary goes to her son to help save the face of the family hosting the wedding. She doesn't want them to be seen as cheapskates or spendthrifts!

A WORD ABOUT JEWISH WEDDINGS THEN AND NOW

If you have ever been to a wedding of Sabbath-observant Jews, the first thing you notice is that men and women sit separately.

Couples rededicating their marriage vows at the Wedding Church in Cana.

Dancing, singing and merrymaking is either with a screen separating the genders (*machitzeh*) or maybe even separate rooms for the celebrants. It's not unusual for two bands, one made up of men and one made up of only women, to perform for their respective genders. Ultra-Orthodox Jewish men regard the singing of women as licentious.

In Jesus' day, celebrants would have a big wedding feast lasting for days involving all of the town. Men and women would sit separately. That is why when Mary went to Jesus when the wine ran out, He said to her, "Woman, why do you involve me?" (John 2:4).

In other words, what are you doing over here with the guys? Mary, ignoring the social faux pas, got down to business. She wanted her son to start to do his stuff. Jesus was reluctant: "My hour has not yet come."

Mary, ignoring her son's remark, told the servants, "Whatever he says to you, do it" (John 2:5).

John took care to mention the stone jars were "the kind used by the Jews for ceremonial washing" (John 2:6). The stone jars were important to the priests who would spend two weeks out of every year serving in the Temple in Jerusalem.

Stone jars, unlike ceramic ones, could be ritually purified, and the water in the jars could be used to purify other utensils.

Servants poured the wine and it was good! The "master of the banquet" even called over the bridegroom and complimented him on its quality. "Everyone brings out the choice wine first and then the cheaper wine after the guests have had too much to drink; but you have saved the best till now" (John 2:10).

SALZBURG IN THE GALILEE

The Franciscan Wedding Church in Cana is one of the most interesting in the Holy Land. Like other churches here, it is built over an older Crusader structure (which was much larger), but unlike any church in Israel, it is modeled after the cathedral in the hometown of the Franciscan priest who designed the structure.

Father Egidius Geissler wanted to celebrate the beauty of the Salzburg Cathedral in Austria. Opened in 1905, the church celebrates the bride and bridegroom in its two towers. The red dome in the middle, binding the two towers, could symbolize the eternal love that binds husband and wife.

The church itself is remarkable not only for its Austrian flavor, but for the archaeological finds in and under the church.

As you enter the church, there is a plastic cover on the right side of the main aisle. It covers a fourth- or fifth-century Aramaic inscription which says:

"Honored be the memory of Joseph, son of Tanchum, son of John, and his sons who have had this altar built."

Is this the same Joseph of Tiberias who commissioned the church at Tabgha? Was this a synagogue-church? It is doubtful that it was a church outright, as the inscription is in Aramaic, the language spoken by Galilean Jews at that time. Either way, remember "holy places stay holy."

NOT JUST THE WEDDING

Cana is famous as the hometown of the disciple Nathanael (John 21:2). Nathanael, who apparently was from a wealthier town than Nazareth, seemed greatly unimpressed by the Messiah's home address:

The next day Jesus decided to leave for Galilee. Finding Philip, he said to him, "Follow me."

Philip, like Andrew and Peter, was from the town of Bethsaida. Philip found Nathanael and told him, "We have found the one Moses wrote about in the Law, and about whom the prophets also wrote—Jesus of Nazareth, the son of Joseph."

"Nazareth! Can anything good come from there?" Nathanael asked. "Come and see," said Philip.

John 1:43-46

MOUNT TABOR

Mount Tabor is the site of several events in the Hebrew Bible. Properly pronounced "tah-BORE" (not "TAY-ber"), the mountain reaches 575 m (1,886 ft) above sea level. Barak gathered his forces here to defeat the Canaanite Sisera at the Prophetess Deborah's order (Judges 4:6, 12-14). Gideon's brothers were killed here (Judges 8:18-19). Mentioned in Chronicles and the Psalm 89, Jeremiah talks of Tabor being "among the mountains" (Jeremiah 46:18). This is no small hill we're talking about here!

Visiting Mt. Tabor

Hours
Sun-Fri 8am to noon; 2-5pm (closed Saturday). Admission free.

How to Get There
Mt. Tabor is situated in the Jezreel Valley northeast of the town of Afula and east of Nazareth.

Bus 350 from Afula is one of the more convenient ways to get there as the bus will drop you off at the bottom of the mountain where the shuttle station is. Five buses daily, 25 min.

Any bus going north on Route 65 from Afula can let you off where Route 7266 meets Route 65, just south of the village of Kfar Tabor.

Walk or drive to the bus station at the end of the Bedouin village of Shibli (the walk should not take longer than an hour from here). From there, shuttles regularly ferry tourists to the top of the mountain as tour buses cannot navigate the narrow road.

However, for many Christians, Mt. Tabor signifies the site of the Transfiguration. Here, Jesus, in Moses' and Elijah's company, is changed. No surprise, the three disciples who witness this Transfiguration are Peter, John and James.

And he said to them, "Truly I tell you, some who are standing here will not taste death before they see that the kingdom of God has come with power." After six days Jesus took Peter, James and John with him and led them up a high mountain, where they were all alone. There he was transfigured before them. His clothes became dazzling white, whiter than anyone in the world could bleach them. And there appeared before them Elijah and Moses, who were talking with Jesus. Peter said to Jesus, "Rabbi, it is good for us to be here. Let us put up three shelters —one for you, one for Moses and one for Elijah." (He did not know what to say, they were so frightened.)

Then a cloud appeared and covered them, and a voice came from the cloud: "This is my Son, whom I love. Listen to him!" Suddenly, when they looked around, they no longer saw anyone with them except Jesus.

As they were coming down the mountain, Jesus gave them orders not to tell anyone what they had seen until the Son of Man had risen from the dead. They kept the matter to themselves, discussing what "rising from the dead" meant.

Mark 9: 1-10

Even though there are two churches here today (one Greek Orthodox, one Roman Catholic), is this the place of the Transfiguration?

The site may have been chosen by the Byzantines, as it is conveniently situated between Nazareth and Capernaum. The early

Mt Tabor: The interior of the church equals, if not surpasses, the exterior.

church father Origen, the Bishop of Caesarea, for example, said this was the place. However, Eusebius, the writer of the *Onomasticon* (the first geographical work of the holy sites in the region of Israel) said that Mount Hermon to the north was the site of the Transfiguration. A much higher mountain (rising 2,814 m/9,233 ft above sea level), it was regarded by the Gentiles living there as akin to Mount Olympus. This is where the local gods dwelt.

Remember that in Jesus' day, a Jewish town was situated on top of Mount Tabor. From there, beacons were lit to announce the new moon and the beginning of festivals. It was so large that General Josephus Flavias was sent there by the "revolutionary" government in Jerusalem to fortify it. If the Transfiguration did indeed happen on Mt. Tabor, why isn't the town mentioned in Scripture? It is hard to imagine the Transfiguration happening in the middle of the town square.

View from Mt. Tabor: Top right is Jewish Upper Nazareth up on the K'sulote Mountains; the town of Deburiya (named after the Prophetess Deborah) bottom right, and the Jezreel Valley.

However, the Franciscan church on top of the mountain (built by the great church architect of the Holy Land, Antonio Barluzzi of Italy) and the view from the peak are well worth the trip.

The Gate of the Winds leads to Mount Tabor.

When you get to the top of the mountain, there's a fork in the road. Left is to the Greek Orthodox Church of Elijah. For the Catholic site, turn right and head through a gatehouse called the Gate of the Winds (*Bab el-Hawa* in Arabic) which was restored in 1897.

The gatehouse was built by the Arab General Al-Adil in the early 13th century CE.

Wait a minute! An *Arab* general? When Mount Tabor falls in to Arab hands after the first Crusader Kingdom is defeated at the Horns of Hattin in 1187 CE, Saladin's successor Al-Adil and son fortify the site. Realizing that they won't be able to hang onto it, they let the Crusaders return to it (under treaty) until it finally falls again to the Muslim general Baibars in 1263. It does not come under Christian control until General Allenby captured the area from the Turks in 1918. However, remains of these walls can still be seen from the hiking trail which begins in front of the gatehouse. A row of cypress trees stands at attention as you approach the parking lot. A metal gate proclaims the site as Franciscan. Restrooms are to the left and a gift shop to the right.

Before you stands the church. As you approach, a modern monastery and guesthouse is on your right. Remains of the Crusader monastery are on the left.

A striking aspect of this church on Mt. Tabor is its majesty. Sitting atop this mountain in the center of the Jezreel Valley, it dominates the landscape.

Perhaps that is the reason it is here at all. The place is not holy to Jews or Muslims. Its importance was strategic. Romans, Jewish rebels, Crusaders, Arab generals, Napoleon, Ottoman Turks and General Allenby all wanted Tabor.

The Jezreel Valley was and is the breadbasket of the Galilee. Whoever has Mt. Tabor has the valley.

The present-day church was built by Barluzzi over the older Crusader one. The style of the church is distinctly Levantine. There is nothing European about it. The Italian architect travelled all over the Middle East, especially to Syria and Lebanon, to create here an edifice that would blend in.

Franciscan Symbol

The Franciscan symbol in the Holy Land is usually two crossed arms over the five-cross "Jerusalem Cross." The cloaked arm represents St. Francis of Assisi and the bare arm represents Jesus. Both hands have stigmata, the hole in the palm caused by the nails being driven through to hold the hands during crucifixion. Our word "stigma" comes from this.

Entering the church, one is dumbstruck by the sheer size of the interior. Take your time to look at this incredible masterpiece.

Take a seat and look up. The roof was originally built with opaque slabs of translucent marble which, unfortunately, proved too fragile and were replaced with heavier pieces.

The "Transfiguration" mosaic on Mt. Tabor. Be sure not to leave the church before entering the side chapels next to the main entrance. The northern one (on the right as you enter) is dedicated to the prophet Elijah.

The church is built in a basilica style with a central nave and aisles on either side. The golden mosaic of the transfiguration dominates the front with Jesus in the center, Moses to his right holding the ten commandments and Elijah holding a scroll on his left. Perhaps the book of the prophets? Peter, John and James regard the scene with wonder. As do we.

The interior of the church is divided into three naves by truly massive pillars. The center nave ends with twelve stairs that descend into the crypt. The other two naves ascend to altars: the right (south) dedicated to the Blessed Sacrament (communion host or bread), the left to the Virgin.

The crypt is built on the older lines of the 11th-century church. The beautiful mosaics on the walls of the crypt represent the nativity, the eucharist, the passion and death, and the resurrection.

Note the ancient (probably 11th-century) mosaic on the floor. To see it, you will have to lift up a carpet that covers it. The projection jutting out of the wall is the remains of a tomb.

Above you, Elijah looks on in wonder as the Lord consumes his offering (on another mount, Mt. Carmel) while the sacrifice to Ba'al is untouched.

Lost in Translation

Notice that Moses is depicted with rays of light coming out of his forehead. This representation, or misrepresentation, of Moses coming down from Mt. Sinai (Exodus 34:29) has spawned centuries of antisemitic lore. When Moses beholds the Almighty, his face shines. In Hebrew, this is written: "his face was radiant." *Karen* in Hebrew can mean radiance, light beam or horn (of an animal). Michaelangelo, among others, have depicted Moses as having horns. This is a result of a mistranslation of the Hebrew into Greek. As a result, Jews were said to have horns, like the devil.

Moses with the law is the subject of the northern chapel. Yet another mountain, Mt. Sinai, reminds us of that similar transfiguration of Moses.

The view from Mt. Tabor is as magnificent as the architecture. Climb the stairs to the right of the entrance (facing the church) and be prepared for one of the best vistas Israel has to offer.

Looking directly down, we see the remains of Al Adil's medieval wall and two of its towers. (By the way, the ruins just under us to the left are the remains of a medieval refectory). Facing east, the Hill of Moreh lies in front.

Below, biblical En Dor, where Saul used the services of a medium (a serious transgression of God's law) to contact the spirit of the prophet Samuel to see if he would be successful against the Philistines (1 Sam 28:6-24). For this, he and his seed were stripped of his kingdom and it would go to the Davidic line.

The highway that runs parallel to the mountain is the ancient highway (today's Route 65) that once connected Damascus to Megiddo and the coast, the Via Maris.

In the distance, note the mountains of Jordan to the left. The mountains to the right are the Gilboa range.

Most visitors only go up the southern staircase. Don't make the same mistake. Upon returning to the church entrance, go up the small flight of stairs to the observation porch on the north side of the church. Though the view is less spectacular, on a clear day Mt. Hermon is visible on the horizon to the left. The Jewish town of Tzfat (Safed), home of Kabbalah, can be seen on the mountains closer still. Kibbutzim (Jewish agricultural communities) dot the rural landscape all round below.

Return to the gate to examine the remains of medieval Benedictine monastery with an oratory, chapel room and refectory.

HIKING PATH: 1.5 HOURS

If you have time and the weather isn't too hot, I recommend taking the hiking path that goes around the top of the mountain. It is especially lovely in the spring when the area is alive with wildflowers including anemone, Persian cyclamen and daisies. The trail begins just before the 13th-century Arab gatehouse and continues in a circular route and lasts about one and a half hours.

ISRAELI HIKING TRAIL BLAZES

All hiking paths in Israel are marked in black, blue, red or green paint markings. Also, purple, orange (historical trails such as the Jesus Trail) or multi-color are used to designate such trails as the Israel Trail and Golan Trail. The colors do not mark the path's difficulty, rather just distinguish between different routes. If a path is marked with blue, orange and white, this signifies the Israel National Trail, which is a 960 km (600 mi) hiking route that crosses the country beginning in the northern border town of Dan and going south all the way to Eilat. Mt. Tabor is included on this spectacular route. For more information, go to www.israel-nationaltrail.com.

OTHER SITES ON THE MOUNTAIN

As you exit the Gate of the Winds, descend the road and turn right to the road that leads to the Greek Orthodox site. About 100 m down the road, you will see a structure kept under lock and key, called the Cave of Melchisedek. The Orthodox believe that this is where the priest-king of Jerusalem (then called Salem) received Abraham (Gen 14:17-20).

Anyway, it is locked, and the key is kept in the Orthodox Church of Elijah. However, both are usually closed to the ordinary tourist.

Father Jerome Murphy-O'Connor, author of *The Holy Land: An Oxford Archaeological Guide* and head of the famous Ecole Biblique et Archeologique Francaise in Jerusalem, calls this tradition regarding Salem bizarre. Perhaps the distance between Tabor and Jerusalem (though both are mountains) seems a little far-fetched for this to be credible. When returning to the main road, you can easily see the remains of the Arab 13th-century towers and walls.

NAIN

The raising of the widow's son in the village of Nain is interesting not only because of the miraculous resurrection, but also because of where the village of Nain is located.

The village of Nain in situated on the hill of Moreh in southern Galilee. Nearby was the village of Shunem (modern-day Sulam), where the prophet Elisha sometimes rested on his journeys from his home in Abel-Meholah in the Jordan Valley on his journeys to Mount Carmel on the northern coast. He stayed with a couple in Shunem who had no children. Elisha blessed the couple and the wife soon gave birth to a son. When their only son dies an untimely early death, Elisha raises the boy to life (2 Kings 4: 8-37).

Jesus does the same thing:

> *Soon afterward, Jesus went to a town called Nain, and his disciples and a large crowd went along with him. As he approached the town gate, a dead person was being carried out—the only son of his mother, and she was a widow. And a large crowd from the town was with her. When the Lord saw her, his heart went out to her and he said, "Don't cry."*

Visiting Nain

The church is not in use, but the family that watches over the church are willing to open the doors for visitors to enter.

How to Get There
Buses 442, 830, 835 and 841 regularly leave the Afula central bus station daily (not on Saturdays) for Nain Junction.
By car, it is a short drive taking Route 65 east from Afula.

Then he went up and touched the bier they were carrying him on, and the bearers stood still. He said, "Young man, I say to you, get up!" The dead man sat up and began to talk, and Jesus gave him back to his mother.

They were all filled with awe and praised God. "A great prophet has appeared among us," they said. "God has come to help his people." This news about Jesus spread throughout Judea and the surrounding country.

Luke 7:11-17

Not only does Jesus perform a miracle similar to Elisha's, but he does it in just about the same place. This would not have been lost on the locals, who certainly would have known about Elisha's miracle years before.

NAIN TODAY

A McDonald's welcomes you today when you turn off Route 65 (north from Afula) to enter the Muslim village of Nain, once an ancient Jewish village bearing the same name.

Getting to the church isn't difficult. As you enter the village, the McDonald's will be on your right. Look straight ahead and the mosque and its minaret will be to the left of the center of the village. Opposite the minaret is the church.

Drive to the center of the village, turn left at the first intersection then continue to the edge of town and turn right and right again.

The family that lives next to the church keeps the keys. They speak only Arabic and a little Hebrew, but will understand that you'd like to visit the site. Please give at least $1 (in shekels) per person. If you've come with a group on a bus, $10 should suffice.

The small Franciscan church in Nain

The church was built in 1881 and is perhaps the least visited edifice of all the sites of Jesus' miracles. However, because there is a very good chance you will be alone on your visit, this is an ideal place to sit for a moment, open the Bible and contemplate the great miracle that was performed here.

The simplicity of the site, devoid of souvenir shops and restaurants perhaps best brings across the significance of where Jesus chose to spread the word of salvation.

The question is, why Nain? As Nain lies just on the other side of the hill from the biblical village of Shunem, the Jews of Jesus' day would have be very aware of the Prophet Elisha's miracle nearby (2 Kings 4:16-37). Jesus' "mirror" miracle of raising a widow's son from the dead would surely be seen by these simple country folk as truly extraordinary and identifying Jesus as a prophet.

WHERE TO STAY

Cana Wedding Guesthouse
(☎04-641-2375; Churches St, Cana; www.canaguesthouse.com) Sami and Suad Bellan run the only guesthouse in Cana out of their sparkling clean home just behind the Catholic church.

Tabor Land Guesthouse
(☎050-544-1972; Kfar Kish; www.taborland.com) Tabor Land is a locally-owned guesthouse near Mount Tabor in the moshav of Kfar Kish. Owner Sarah Yeffet cultivates a peaceful herb garden and keeps the spacious grounds spotless.

Hooha's Cyclists House
(☎054-807-0524;Kfar Tavor;www.hooha.co.il) Hooha's offers a unique atmosphere in their accommodations near Mount Tabor. Though catering mainly to cyclists, it's a luxurious and friendly choice by foot or car as well. High-quality mountain bikes available for rent.

WHERE TO EAT

The main street of Cana has many good and inexpensive restaurants, mainly serving hummus, falafel, shwarma and other typical fare. Try **New York Pizza**, just by the turn to Churches Street, for surprisingly good American-style pizza.

Falafel Golani in Afula (not far from Nain) may just be one of the best falafel stands in all of Israel. Located opposite the police station in the center of town, it is only a short walk from the central bus station. May just be the best 15NIS meal in the country. Be sure to put plenty of the available salads, humus, tehina and spicy hot sauce on the sandwich.

Falafel Golani (6 Weizman Street ☎04-659-0558. Open daily 9am-9pm; Fri until 3pm; closed Saturdays and Jewish holidays.)

There is a McDonald's on the main junction into Nein, but the **Sahara restaurant** (☎04-676-7673) is worth a visit. Better than the standard Middle Eastern restaurants of the area, Sahara offers grilled meats and fish. Sahara's specialty is *mansaf* made with pine nuts rice and lamb, but the baked lamb in thick, tasty bread is a local favorite. Call ahead.

SIDE TRIP: MOUNT HERMON

THE MORE LIKELY SITE OF THE TRANSFIGURATION

Though Mount Tabor, the traditional site of the Transfiguration, has mostly been ruled out by most Christian scholars as the historical location, it is still well worth visiting.

So where is the real mountain? Most scholars say Mt. Hermon.

Mt. Hermon has more of a "biblical pedigree" than Tabor. Mt. Tabor is mentioned only in Judges 4 as a place where Deborah stationed Barak and his ten thousand soldiers to swoop down upon the hapless Sisera and his army.

However, Mount Hermon is praised for its beauty:
> *Come with me from Lebanon, my bride, come with me from Lebanon. Descend from the crest of Amana, from the top of Senir, the summit of Hermon, from the lions' dens and the mountain haunts of leopards.*

Song of Songs 4:8

Visiting Mt. Hermon

How to Get There
Infrequent bus service to the Golan Heights means you'll need a rental car for this trip.

What to See and Do
Visit a Druze town, such as Magdal Shams or visit the small ski resort on the mount.

See p. 173-177 for information on nearby sites Dan and Cesarea Philipi (Banias)

The snow-capped peak of Mount Hermon.

And for its majesty:
My soul is downcast within me;
therefore I will remember you
from the land of the Jordan,
the heights of Hermon—from Mount Mizar.

Psalms 42:6

Mentioned in Deuteronomy (3:8-9), Mount Hermon rates a geographic explanation on how it is named by other peoples. The name "Hermon" comes from the Arabic *Haram*, meaning "holy" or "sanctuary." The mountain is indeed associated with holiness and greatness. The tallest of all the mountains in the Holy Land at 9,166 ft (2,814 m), the mountain range is also a giver of life. Composed of ancient limestone and dolomite rock, the mountain absorbs all the vast amounts of rain and snow that fall there. Percolating through the layers of stone, the water eventually bursts forth at the base in various places in the form of springs.

The famous mosaic of loaves and fishes at
Tabgha. Where is the fifth loaf? See p. 131.

Jesus' Ministry at Capernaum

Capernaum
Tabgha
Primacy of Peter Church
Mount of Beatitudes
Jesus Boat

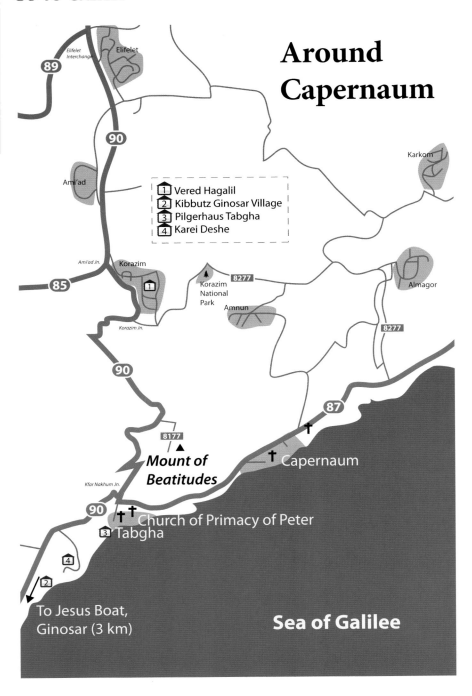

Around Capernaum

Karkom

Elifelet
Interchange
Elifelet

89

90

Ami'ad

1	Vered Hagalil
2	Kibbutz Ginosar Village
3	Pilgerhaus Tabgha
4	Karei Deshe

Ami'ad Jn.
Korazim

85

1

8277

Korazim
National
Park

Almagor

Amnun

8277

Korazim Jn.

90

8277

87

8177

▲

*Mount of
Beatitudes*

† Capernaum

Kfar Nakhum Jn.

90

†† Church of Primacy of Peter

3 Tabgha

4

2

To Jesus Boat,
Ginosar (3 km)

Sea of Galilee

TOUR 4 SNAPSHOT

Sites
Capernaum, Mount of Beatitudes, Church of the Primacy of Saint Peter, Tabgha

Length
4-5 hours

Type of Tour
While it is possible to drive between everything, the sites are close enough together that I recommend walking between them to enjoy the fresh air and views of the Sea of Galilee.

Highlights
Views of the Sea of Galilee from the Mount of Beatitudes, mosaics at Tabgha, peaceful shoreline, Capernaum synagogue

TOUR 4 INTRODUCTION

After his baptism by John, Jesus leaves Nazareth and goes north to the shores of the Sea of Galilee and there begins his ministry. This tour follows in his footsteps and begins in Capernaum, Jesus' home base. The tour continues west to the site of the miracle of the feeding of the 5,000 (Tabgha) and the Church of the Primacy of Saint Peter to walk along the shores of this beautiful lake. Next, the tour continues upward (the Sea of Galilee is the world's lowest body of fresh water—more than 212 m [696 ft] below sea level!) to the magnificent site of the Mount of the Beatitudes to enjoy a panoramic view of where Jesus felt at home.[1]

The walk from Nazareth to Capernaum would have taken more than one full day. Whether Jesus and his disciples would have walked north and at Zippori taken the Netofa Valley route east or, the more logical route, walk down into the Jezreel Valley and follow, more or less, today's Route 65 north to Kfar Tavor and then east on Route 767 and then head north to Capernaum, we'll never know. Today's Jesus Trail (see page 108) omits the latter, but Christian scholar Dr. James Fleming favors it. If you have a car, I suggest taking Route 767, as it is more logical and more scenic than the Netofa Valley route, which is not navigable by car.

This would be a good time to stop the car at a popular observation point just past the roundabout that connects Routes 767 and 768. Here, the northern Jordan Valley stretches in front of you with the hills of the Gilead (present-day Jordan) on the right and the Golan Heights and the Sea of Galilee to your left.

Continue the journey to Route 90 and turn left (north), keeping the lake on the right all the way to Capernaum.

---

1   According to the NIV translation of Mark 2:1.

CAPERNAUM

Capernaum is a hugely important place in the life of Jesus. He moved there from Nazareth, and it became his home during his ministry in the Galilee (Matthew 4:13; Luke 4:31).

LEAVING NAZARETH

The gospel of Matthew reports that Jesus lefts his hometown of Nazareth and went to Capernaum:

Leaving Nazareth, he went and lived in Capernaum, which was by the lake in the area of Zebulun and Naphtali - to fulfill what was said through the prophet Isaiah:

the land of Zebulun and the land of Naphtali, but in the future he will honor Galilee of the nations, by the Way of the Sea, beyond the Jordan—

The people walking in darkness have seen a great light; on those living in the land of deep darkness a light has dawned.

Matthew 4:13-16

Using the city as a home base, Jesus then recruited the first of his disciples, Simon Peter and his brother Andrew:

Capernaum

It's the place where Jesus recruited most of his disciples (Mark 2:13-14, 3:13-19; Matt. 9:9; 10:2-4, 4: 18-22; Luke 6:12-16) and performed miracles (healing Peter's mother-in-law and others, Matt. 8:14-17; the paraplegic [so many wanted to be healed that the poor man was lowered through a hole made in the thatch and mud roof], Mark 2:1-5; the Centurion's servant, Matt. 8:5-13; and the resurrection of the daughter of Jairus, Mark 5:21-43). Yet, the people did not repent and Jesus foretold its destruction (Matt. 11:23-24).

115

Visiting Capernaum

Hours
8am to 4:45pm daily

Entrance Fee
3NIS per person for the archeological site

Remember, modest dress is required for all the sites today. That especially means no shorts or tank tops.

How to Get There
From Tiberias and the south:
Take Route 90 north to Capernaum Junction and turn right. Route 87 begins here.
From the North:
Take Route 90 south and turn left at Capernaum Junction. Follow the road as it twists left. You will pass Tabgha Church and the Church of the Primacy. Not to worry; you will be coming back on this road. Keep driving until the brown sign on the right that will lead you to the site. Don't park in the parking lot on the right. That is for buses. Continue through the narrow (and I mean narrow!) gate and park there. Restrooms are found here, too.

While walking by the Sea of Galilee, he saw two brothers, Simon (who is called Peter) and Andrew his brother, casting a net into the sea, for they were fishermen. And he said to them, "Follow me, and I will make you fishers of men."

Matt. 4:18-19

He then recruited two more, James and John, sons of Zebedee. This was quite impressive, since their father owned his boat and probably used hired hands to man it. James and John left a sure inheritance to follow their Rabbi.

The modern Franciscan church at Capernaum is built over St. Peter's house.

WHY IS CAPERNAUM IMPORTANT?

We now know, thanks to archaeological evidence, that Capernaum was larger than the other villages along the Sea of Galilee. The town was also on the main road (called the Via Maris) connecting the coastal plain and valleys with Damascus and beyond. Today, the modern Trans-Israel Highway, Route 6, roughly follows this ancient route. A border town, Capernaum sat on the eastern border of Herod Antipas' kingdom and the Decapolis, a loose confederation of ten pagan cities directly ruled by Rome. Therefore, it had a tax collector and a century of Roman soldiers to ensure the emperor got his due. The officer in charge of the soldiers was probably the righteous or "god-fearing" Gentile who donated money to build the synagogue. The tax collector is, of course, Matthew, the last disciple called:

As Jesus went on from there, he saw a man named Matthew sitting at the tax collector's booth. "Follow me," he told him, and Matthew got up and followed him.

Matt 9:9

Fishing was the main industry in the area. There were seven anchorages in Capernaum in the first century. All the other towns had only one, which means when Jesus chose Capernaum as a home base, it was a thriving fishing and trade center.

Jesus chose Capernaum because of the people who lived there. They were simple fishermen and farmers, tax collectors (sometimes called "publicans" or contractors, employed by Rome and about as popular then as the IRS) and those living on the edge of society.

The tabernacle in the desert or a moveable Torah ark? Part of the impressive limestone frieze that ornamented the Byzantine-era synagogue at Capernaum.

Word Origins

Capernaum means "the town of Nahum." We don't know who this Nahum was, but the early church father Origen believed the name derived from the Hebrew noun *nahum*, meaning "consolation."

Perhaps there is another reason Jesus came to Capernaum. Christian scholar Dr. James Fleming theorized that as a result of his cousin John the Baptist's execution by Herod Antipas, king of Galilee, Jesus "felt the heat" and went to a border town so he could make a fast getaway to the Decapolis should Herod Antipas consider him a threat.

Today, this area is serenely lovely, with its churches and kept gardens. However, 2,000 years ago, it was a place of political turmoil and a cauldron of discontent with Rome.

Dr. James Fleming reckons that the Jews of first-century Galilee were the most taxed people in the Roman Empire. Owing to the fact that even though they were barely eking out a living, they not only had to pay the heavy taxes to Rome, but also paid the half-shekel Temple tax and bought suitable animals for sacrifice when they took their yearly pilgrimages to Jerusalem. This made Jesus all the more sensitive to their plight when he saw how the priests at the Temple were overcharging the pilgrims. Seething with anger, he started a minor riot in the Temple precincts earning him the enmity of this very lucrative, priestly-lead monopoly.

As you enter the site, a gold-painted statue of Simon Peter dominates the scene. Go right to the limestone lintel stones that decorated the 4th- or 5th-century synagogue. You'll see a collection of geometric forms, eagles and flowers. These decorations are some of the most beautiful and unusual for a synagogue of that era. There is also something else: a curious cart of some sort on wheels.

What exactly is this wheeled contraption? Is it the ark of the tabernacle of the children of Israel? Some have proposed that the wooden cabinet holding the Torah scrolls in the ancient synagogue had such a thing to move around during services and lock up later. Dr. Moti Aviam, a leading expert on ancient synagogues, says that the Torah was kept in a permanent ark, probably made of wood, next to the entrance. This way, the worshippers would be facing Jerusalem when praying. So ark of the tabernacle it is. Notice also the flowers, pomegranates, grapes and other decorations which adorned the structure.

The site's remains of the 3rd- to 6th-century city of Capernaum was excavated by Franciscan archaeologists. The two most im-

The sign in front states that a later synagogue was built on an earlier, 1st-century building, probably paid for by the Roman centurion (Luke 7: 1-10).

portant finds in the town are the Byzantine octagonal church over the house of Peter and the white synagogue.

In front now is the new very modern chapel that sits on top of the church that was built over the house of Simon Peter (or likely the house of his wife's family, as he was from Bethsaida). The new chapel obscures a really good view of this most important church. You can enter the chapel and look down through a glass floor to get another view (though certainly not a better one) of the eight-sided basilica. After a moment's reflection in the chapel, turn left after descending the stairs and look at the sign that is posted on the other side of the fence that explains what you are seeing.

Very little remains here to see, but the sign on the left explains the four stages of the church's development from a simple home to an eight-sided basilica.[2] The ruins to the left, in front of the synagogue, are the remains of the city from the 4th-5th century CE. Most archaeologists agree that the white synagogue was built over an older one, which perhaps was financed by the centurion whose son was healed by Jesus (Matt 8).

CAPERNAUM SYNAGOGUE

The large white structure that dominates the site is the synagogue that Jesus probably didn't teach in, but he probably taught in an older synagogue built on this site.

Consisting of three parts: a central prayer hall (20.4x18.7 m or 70x61 ft), a court to the east (11.3 m or 37 ft wide at the front) and a front porch that faced Jerusalem, the synagogue was surrounded by streets on each side which necessitated entry from the sides, not directly into the building from the front.

---

2   One explanation why there are many eight-sided basilicas is because the eight sides represent Easter, the "eighth day" marking a new creation.

Why not Bar Mitzvahs?

At the time of Jesus, males came of age at 13 and were obligated to take on the responsibilities of an adult. The actual celebration of this would not be practiced until well into the 14th century CE. More than likely, girls who reached the age of 12 (the age when Jewish girls today celebrate a bat mitzvah) were either betrothed or married, as this is about when they reached sexual maturity. They married young back then!

The date palm, not the Star of David, was the recognized symbol of the Judeans (Jews) in the ancient world.

When approaching the synagogue, be sure to see the sign that illustrates what it looked like 1,500 years ago.

Before going up the steps, notice the difference between the black basalt rock foundation and the white limestone of the synagogue itself. What can explain the not-so-perfect seam?

Most experts agree that the black basalt foundation was indeed part of the earlier 1st-century BCE synagogue. When the town grew in importance and wealth, a newer (and larger) synagogue was constructed over the site of the original that could have been damaged in an earthquake. Was this new synagogue the main synagogue of the Jewish Christians that would have gravitated to their master's home base?

Another theory that explains this curious discrepancy is that the Jews were unable to build a new synagogue here due to new harsh, anti-Jewish laws from Constantinople. To go around these new restrictions, they went to a deserted Jewish village further west in Galilee where the local stone is white limestone (here it is black basalt), took apart the local synagogue and reconstructed it here in Capernaum, thus circumventing the laws forbidding the construction of new synagogues.

When entering any site in the Holy Land, take a moment and look up! There are three entrances to the synagogue. Look at the lintel above the center door. Date palm trees decorate the entrance. The symbolism here is important. The date tree was the "star of David" in the ancient world. It was the symbol of the Jewish people. The Judean date was famous throughout the Roman Empire as being particularly big and sweet. When Judea fell to Vespasian in 70 CE, he minted a coin portraying Judea as a woman under a date palm as a symbol of the two main spoils of that war— slaves and date plantations.

The synagogue was construced in basilica style with three entrances and a center nave with an aisle on each side. What is missing is a mosaic floor that usually decorated synagogues like these in the Galilee. We can see examples in Hamat Tiberias, Zippori, Beit Alpha, etc.

Note the benches jutting from the walls and the eastern side room. The wooden cupboard that held the Torah scrolls were probably situated next to the entrance so as to permit the worshippers to face Jerusalem while praying.

In Jesus' time, there was no fixed time for prayer. Indeed, when the Temple in Jerusalem was still standing, prayers were only recited in Jerusalem.

Jews probably assembled on the Sabbath to read from the Bible and study under a learned sage (see Luke 4:14). Synagogues were the cultural centers of the day where Jews not only met to read

GREEK ORTHODOX CHURCH
OF THE SEVEN APOSTLES

Hours: Mon-Sat 8am-5pm
Entrance Fee: None; please leave some shekels out of courtesy

Most tours go to the archelogical site of Capernaum which is in the hands of the Franciscan order. It's worth the side trip to the view the red-domed Greek Orthodox church of the Seven Apostles.

Built in 1931, the church is dedicated to the seven apostles (Simon called Peter, Thomas called Didymus, Nathanael from Cana in Galilee, the sons of Zebedee, and "two other disciples"). Situated on the part of the city probably from the late Byzantine era (8th century), the church is located on an ancient quay that served the city.

Note the iconography that depicts, among other things, Jesus' descent into hell on the Saturday between Good Friday and Easter Sunday in order to bring the souls of Adam, Eve, Abraham and other saints of the Hebrew Bible to heaven.

from the law, but also held weddings and town meetings in times of turmoil.

You will notice two columns opposite the main entrance. One has a Greek inscription and the other is inscribed in Aramaic (which looks like Hebrew). The Greek inscription reads: "Herod, son of Mo[ni]mos, and Justus his son, together with (his) children, erected this column." The one in Aramaic reads: "Yochanon made this column. May he be blessed."

Walk across to the side room. On your right as you enter note the graffiti on the floor. These games are similar to the ones found in Zippori. Perhaps while the parents were praying on Saturdays, the younger children here were passing the time playing these games.

There is a shady spot with benches next to the synagogue which is an ideal place for silent contemplation or for a lesson. Be sure to see the exhibition of ancient olive presses beyond the fence, to the right of the exit when leaving.

For those who might not have a chance for a good view of the Sea of Galilee, to the right of the entrance to the upper chapel lies a wonderful spot to take in the beauty of this very special lake. Just walk past the gate and have cameras at the ready.

TABGHA CHURCH

MULTIPLICATION OF THE LOAVES AND FISHES

Take note that we pass the Church of the Primacy north of Tabgha Church and some interesting ruins on the opposite side of the road. We'll get back to these later.

When the Lazarist[3] fathers of the German Association of the Holy Land built their pilgrims' hostel on the northwest shores of the Sea of Galilee in 1889, little did they know that 33 years later ancient mosaics would be discovered. These mosaics were the floor of a church. One of the these would prove to be the most famous Christian mosaics in the Holy Land.

The site was identified as the Church of Saint Joseph. This Joseph was a converted Jew from Tiberias who built the church here to commemorate the feeding of the five thousand.

---

3 An order of vowed priests who revere St. Vincent de Paul as their founder.

Church of the Multiplication of Loaves and Fishes from the courtyard.

Visiting Tabgha

Hours
Daily 8am to 4:45pm. Closed on Sunday. Entrance free.
☎ 04-670-0180

How to Get There
From Capernaum, take Route 87 west for 2 km. From Tiberias, take Route 90 north to Route 87.

Taking the five loaves and the two fish and looking up to heaven, he gave thanks and broke the loaves. Then he gave them to his disciples to distribute to the people. He also divided the two fish among them all.

They all ate and were satisfied, and the disciples picked up twelve basketfuls of broken pieces of bread and fish. The number of the men who had eaten was five thousand.

Mark 6:41-44

Called *Et-Tabgha* in Arabic, this is a corruption of the Greek *heptapegon* which means "seven springs." The entire northwest corner of the lake is inundated with geothermal saline springs, some of which lie on the lake bed. This is the reason why the fishing in this area is so good. The St. Peter's fish is a warmwater fish and is attracted to the warm springs bubbling from the bottom of the lake.

Despite the profusion of saline springs, Josephus describes the area's rich agricultural productivity. Today, the area is surrounded with banana, olive and mango groves which give the visitors an almost tropical feeling as they wind their way between the chapels, shore and ruins. Unfortunately, lake water is used for irrigation, further depleting the water level which is already dangerously low.

PILGRIM'S PROMENADE

Heed my advice and take advantage of the "pilgrims' promenade" that connects the Orthodox site of Capernaum to the Franciscan site and continues west to Tabgha.

This beautiful walkway is an absolute must. Best done in the morning during the warmer months, this 2 1/4 km (1.5 mi) stroll is the best way to relive Jesus' ministry along this tranquil lake. Dotted along the path are rest stops. These are the perfect places to read Scripture that deals with the Sea of Galilee. For example: The calming of the storm (Mark 4: 35-41; Matt 8:23-27; Luke 8:22-25); Walking on the water (Mark 6:47-52; Matt 14:27-33; John 6:15-21).

The "Pilgrims' Promenade" that connects the churches at Tabgha to Capernaum

What makes the Church of the Multiplication of Loaves and Fishes unique is the fact that the early Christians constructed a 4th-5th century CE Byzantine church that celebrated the site of the feeding of the five thousand.

Imagine traveling through time and arriving at the year 500 CE. This is the type of church you would encounter in the Holy Land. However, the original magnificent structure was destroyed in the 7th century, probably during the Persian (Parthian) invasion of the Holy Land in 614 CE, when almost all Byzantine churches were destroyed. Unlike most sites where this happened, the Crusaders did not find and rebuild the church.

In front of the entrance is an olive press. The stone roller was used to crush the olives, and then the paste was put into woven dough-nut-shaped baskets which were stacked on a press using a screw that pressed the oil out of the paste. The basalt stone bottom part is on display here.

Built in 1982, this is one of the newest churches in the Holy Land. It is to the Benedictine order's credit that the present church was built to conform to the original church's mosaic floor. However, the builders did not only stick to the original design of the church itself, they also were very keen to preserve aspects of early Byzantine churches.

Take, for instance, the large, open courtyard. In sheer size, it is almost as large as the church itself. Why were such courtyards common in early Byzantine times? The answer is where the church was situated and the function that this large courtyard served.

In early Byzantine times, from the late 4th century well into the 6th, most of the populace in this area were not born Christians. They were Jews, Jewish Christians and pagans. Some of these people were interested in seeing what was going on in this magnificent building on Sunday mornings. They would congregate in the courtyard and observe the service through the three open doors of the basilica-styled building. Should one observer be consistent in their visits, the bishop (or other clergyman) would notice them.

Remember that at this period of time, Mass would last hours. Casual observers would probably come and go, but someone truly interested in this new religion would stay and return again. Perhaps after one service, they would be asked if they wanted to join the community of believers and if they answered in the affirmative, they would be baptized there.

However, the round structure in the middle of the courtyard is not a baptistry. It is a **cantharus**. What is a cantharus, you ask? Well, a cantharus is a water fountain used to wash before entering the church. This practice survives today, but in Islam! The church itself, even though it is run by a Catholic order, is devoid of any statuary. Only a few icons and a gold sequined cross ornament this stately presence.

The real stars here are the mosaics. Starting counter-clockwise on our left (north), we see a large bird which is fighting a rock hyrax sporting a red collar. As we progress towards the left side of the altar[4] we see an aquatic scene with many species of birds we can actually identify. Red crested ducks, herons, snipes, barnacle geese, stone curlews and a flamingo killing a water snake adorn this magnificent piece of art. The transept to the right (south) is dominated by a stone column with Greek letters carved on it.

This is called a **Nilometer**, and it was used to measure how much the Nile River flooded in order to tax the farmers. The more the Nile rose, the more it flooded, thus allowing more land to be culti-

---

4   The areas to the left and right of the altar are called transepts.

Hyrax and crane mosaics at Tabgha.

vated and hence taxed by its rulers. Clever, huh? The question is: what's a Nile scene doing in a church on the Sea of Galilee?

Nilometers are common in the Holy Land. We saw one at Zippori. Perhaps the most famous Christian mosaic in the Holy Land is the one directly in front of the altar. A good tour guide will ask their group, "Where is the fifth loaf? Scriptures tell us there were five loaves."

The mosaic lies under the altar. During Mass, the priest raises the communion wafer above his head and blesses it. The fifth loaf is the Eucharist. Another explanation is found in John 6:35: "*Then Jesus declared, "I am the bread of life. Whoever comes to me will never go hungry, and whoever believes in me will never be thirsty."* Jesus is the fifth loaf.

The altar itself is built over the stone on which Jesus performed the miracle. The stone used to be much bigger, but generations of Christian pilgrims hacking away at it to bring a piece back home has reduced it to its present size.

Another great thing about this church is that all Christians— Protestants, Catholics, Orthodox, and others can feel welcome here. At the time of writing, the German brothers were in the process of building a new monastery.

If you have come with a car, leave it at the parking lot of the Tabgha Church and walk out to the main road (Route 87) and walk just a few meters uphill and look at the remains on the other side of the road. These are the remains of an earlier church called the Church of the Sermon on the Mount. Built at the end of the 4th-century CE, this was also probably destroyed by the Parthians in 614 CE or by the Muslims 24 years later. The present church up the hill is on the Mount of Beatitudes (see p. 135).

> When they had finished eating, Jesus said to Simon Peter, "Simon, son of John, do you truly love me more than these?" "Yes, Lord," he said, "you know that I love you." Jesus said, "Take care of my sheep."
>
> John 21:15-16

THE CHURCH OF PRIMACY OF PETER

> When they landed, they saw a fire of burning coals there with fish on it, and some bread...Jesus came, took the bread and gave it to them, and did the same with the fish.
>
> John 21:9-13

This simple chapel built in 1933 by the Franciscan Order marks the spot where the risen Jesus met the disciples for a meal. The altar of this basalt stone edifice is called the *Mensa Christi*, the "table of Christ." The remains of an earlier 4th-century church are visible on three sides, but the structure was much larger. It was destroyed only in the late Crusader period (13th century CE).

Visiting the Church of St. Peter's Primacy

Hours
Entrance free, open daily 8am to 5pm

Outside the church, cuts in the limestone testify to quarrying here. Nearer the shore, the remains of heart-shaped stones, sometimes called "the thrones of the apostles," lie next to the modern chapel. Usually used in corner colonnades, they were perhaps reposi-

The Church of the Primacy of Peter as seen from the shore, but a recent drought and water overuse have changed things. These pilgrims would have been knee-deep in water in 2003.

tioned here in a later building. The true wonder of this place is the tranquil setting where you can experience the Sea of Galilee close up. It seems to invite you to shed your shoes and wade into the cool waters.

There are places to the left of the church to sit on the shore and read, sing hymns, reflect and share in a very special moment. Of note are the bronze doors of the chapel, one dedicated to Pope Paul VI, who visited Israel in 1964, and the other to Pope John Paul II, who came in March 2000.

Mount of Beatitudes

MOUNT OF BEATITUDES

*Now when Jesus saw the crowds, he went up on a mountainside
and sat down. His disciples came to him, and he began to teach
them. He said:*

*"Blessed are the poor in spirit for theirs is the kingdom of heaven.
Blessed are those who mourn, for they will be comforted.
Blessed are the meek, for they will inherit the earth.
Blessed are those who hunger and thirst for righteousness,
  for they will be filled.
Blessed are the merciful, for they will be shown mercy.
Blessed are the pure in heart, for they will see God.
Blessed are the peacemakers, for they will be called
  children of God."*

Matthew 5:1-9

These eight sentences rendered in truly poetic English by the
translators of the King James version of the New Testament (the
English poet John Milton among them) are perhaps the best
known of Jesus' teachings. Here, on top of a hill overlooking the
Sea of Galilee and the Plain of Genneserat, is the traditional site of
the Sermon on the Mount.

The site is unlike many churches in the Holy Land as no older
remains were found nearby. The lovely church built by Antonio
Barluzzi in 1938 is run by Franciscan nuns. Built with local basalt
stone, the limestone-trimmed arches reflect the waves of the Sea
of Galilee. The columns are of travertine, a common material
used in Rome in the 1920s and 30s.

Beautiful is the byword here. "Beatitudes" comes from the Latin
beati which means "blessed." Though no archaeological remains
point to this location as the "mount" of the Sermon of the Mount,
it is a great spot to enjoy a view of the Sea of Galilee (best seen

Visiting the Mount of Beatitudes

Hours
Mon–Sat 8–11:30am; 2:30–4:40 pm

Entrance Fee
10NIS per car; 20NIS for large van or SUV

How to Get There
Mount of Beatitudes in located on Route 90 between Capernaum Junction and the town of Rosh Pina. Buses 63, 841 and 963 stop at the entrance from Tiberias. There is a 1 km walk from the road to the entrance. There is also an unmarked hiking trail that begins on Route 87 just past the Church of the Primacy of St. Peter. Cross the road and walk past the church compound until you get to a metal staircase. Continue up the dirt path until you reach the paved road the leads to the church.

from the parking lot for buses). The Iberian pilgrim Egeria mentions a cave above Tabgha as the site of Jesus' famous sermon. The cave lies on Route 87 just opposite the entrance to The Primacy of St. Peter's Church.

A Franciscan convent stands opposite the church. Behind the gift shop is the guesthouse for pilgrim groups. Inside the church, the first few words of each of the Beatitudes is written in Latin on the stained glass windows in the dome above.

Quiet, simple and yet striking in the natural beauty of the surrounding gardens, the Mount of the Beatitudes gives the visitor an opportunity for quiet reflection, prayer and solace. Be sure to stroll around the church. It is best to visit in the afternoon with the sun behind you to get the best view of the lake and the surrounding area of Jesus' ministry.

SIDE TRIP:
YIGAL ALLON MUSEUM: THE "JESUS BOAT"

Now that you have taken in sites near Capernaum, take Route 90 and travel to Kibbutz Ginosar and the artifact dubbed "the Jesus Boat." In 1986, there was a severe drought in the Galilee. Water levels of Lake Kinneret dropped to their lowest levels in modern times. As a result, a most amazing thing was found—a 2,000 year old fishing boat!

After paying the entrance fee, ask the cashier to play the short film. Before you go in the exhibit, take a look at the model ship in front of the entrance. Prof. Jerome Hall of the University of California, San Diego, one of the world's leading experts on this boat, is of the opinion that it had no main sail, but the rest of the model is fairly accurate.

Albert Einstein said that "Coincidences were God's way of staying anonymous."

Here are a few coincidences regarding this most remarkable find:
1. It was found by Jewish fishermen.
2. When it was found, a double-rainbow appeared in the sky (pictures of the rainbow are exhibited on the wall next to the boat).
3. The area archaeologist on call just happened to be a nautical archaeologist, Dr. Shelley Wachsman, specializing in ancient ships—a rarity in the archaeological world.
4. There are 12 different types of wood in the boat.

Literally "stuck in the mud" for almost two thousand years, the boat was preserved almost intact—the mud acting as an insulating buffer preventing disintegration.

After a frantic two-week rescue dig, the ship was placed in a bath of heated chemicals designed to preserve the ancient wood. The results are on display here.

A self-service restaurant, restrooms and gift shop are on the premises. This is also a great place to catch a tour of the lake as the main departure point is just outside the glass doors next to the entrance of the boat exhibit.

A SEA OF GALILEE CRUISE AND A ST. PETER'S FISH LUNCH

No tour of the Galilee is complete without a cruise on the Sea of Galilee on one of the special wooden boats made for the purpose of taking visitors on an hour-long tour of this very special body of water.

Two main tour companies specialize in this: **Kibbutz Ein Gev** on the Eastern shore of the lake was founded in 1936. They operate the **Kinneret Sailing Company.** This is my first recommendation because you can purchase a combined ticket of the cruise and lunch at Ein Gev's famous fish restaurant. Call the Kinneret company at ☎04-675-8008 to reserve a place on one of the cruises.

The restaurant has been making their famous St. Peter's fish, (half-fried/ half-grilled) for over 50 years. Among Israelis, there is a general consensus that nobody does it better. A St. Peter's fish meal costs 77NIS plus tip.

Holyland Sailing also books cruises. ☎04-672-3006/7, www.jesusboats.com, located on the marina in Tiberias. Be sure to book the cruise at the latest by 1pm, as the lake tends to get choppy in the afternoon.

Visiting Yigal Allon Museum

Hours
Sat-Thurs 8am-5pm; Fri 8am-4pm;
☎ 04-672-7700

Entrance Fee
20NIS for Adults; 15NIS for children

Located in Kibbutz Ginosar on the northeastern shore of the Sea of Galilee.

Any bus going north from Tiberias can drop you off at Ginosar Junction, including bus 841, 450, 59, 52, and 63.

www.jesusboatmuseum.com

The Ancient Galilee Boat. Too many coincidences!

If you are with a rented car, leave it at **Kibbutz Ginosar** at the **Yigal Allon Center**, and take a cruise that will return you there.

If you are backpacking, on a bus, or have more than one vehicle, book the cruise from the dock at Ginosar to Kibbutz Ein Gev and have lunch at the restaurant. For those who aren't crazy about fish, Ein Gev offers a varied menu from pizza to salads.

For those who are using public transportation, bus #22 from Tiberias will get you to Ein Gev and back, and also take you to Kursi (see p. 162).

WHERE TO STAY

Vered Hagalil

(☎04-693-5785; Korazim Junction, www.veredhagalil.com) Vered Hagalil is just up Route 90 from the Mount of Beatitudes. It is one of the thirteen sites in Israel listed in the book "1,000 Places to See Before You Die." Started by a former Chicagoan who jumped into France on D-Day, Vered Hagalil hosts a dude ranch. A great way to see the Galilee is on horseback tours given here. The cabins provide great views of the sea, and the on-site restaurant is excellent. Cabins that can hold a family of five begin at $140 per night with breakfast but can go up to $295 during high season (October and May).

Kibbutz Ginosar Village

(☎04-670-0320; www.ginosar.co.il) Kibbutz Ginosar runs the pricier Nof Ginosar Hotel, as well as more affordable Ginosar Village cabins and suites. Good choice for families, with access to a beach on the Sea of Galilee.

Pilgerhaus Tabgha

(☎04-670-0100; www.heilig-land-verein.de)
This historic German guesthouse dates back to 1889. The beautiful grounds are conveniently located close to the churches on the northern shore of the Sea of Galilee.

Karei Deshe

(☎02-594-5633; Tabgha; www.iyha.org.il)
A member of the International Youth Hostel Federation, Karei Deshe is located right on the Sea of Galilee close to Tabgha with both private and dorm rooms. Good value with beautiful grounds, but be sure to book as early as large groups often monopolize the rooms during high season.

WHERE TO EAT

There is a small, self-service restaurant at the Jesus Boat Museum. Near Capernaum there is a small fish restaurant on the shore of the Sea of Galilee. In nearby Migdal there are a few small restaurants and sandwich stands. The accommodations mentioned here also serve dinner. A packed lunch to enjoy on the shore is recommended.

The Jordan River at Bethsaida

Around the Sea of Galilee

Jordan River & Bethsaida
Korazim
Kursi
Susita
Yardenit

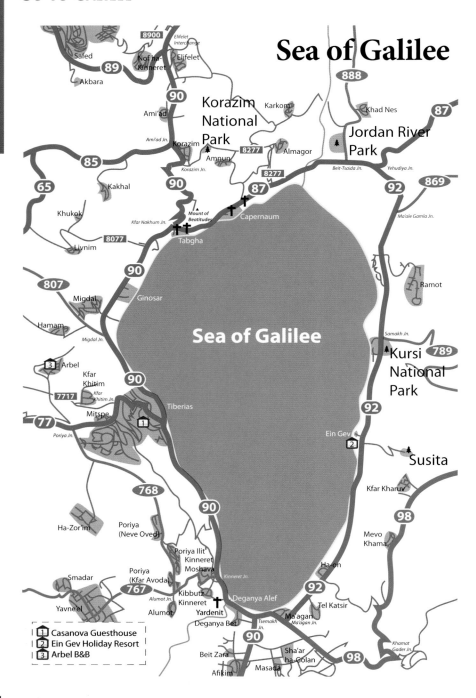

Sea of Galilee

Safed · 89 · Nof ha-Kinneret · Elifelet · 8900 · Elifelet Interchange · 888 · Akbara

Ami'ad · 90 · Korazim National Park · Karkom · Khad Nes · 87

Ami'ad Jn. · Korazim · 8277 · Almagor · Jordan River Park

85 · Korazim Jn. · Amnun · 8277 · Beit-Tsaida Jn. · Yehudiya Jn. · 92 · 869

65 · Kakhal · 90 · 87 · Ma'ale Gamla Jn.

Khukok · Kfar Nakhum Jn. · Mount of Beatitudes · Capernaum

8077 · Tabgha · Ramot

Livnim

807 · Migdal · Ginosar

Hamam · Migdal Jn. · **Sea of Galilee** · Samakh Jn.

3 · Arbel · Kfar Khitim · 90 · Kursi National Park · 789

7717 · Kfar Khitim Jn. · Tiberias · 92

77 · Mitspe · 1 · Ein Gev · 2 · Susita

Poriya Jn. · Kfar Kharuv

768 · 98

Ha-Zor'im · Poriya (Neve Oved) · 90 · Mevo Khama

Poriya Ilit · Kinneret Moshava · Ha-on

Smadar · Poriya (Kfar Avoda) · Alumot Jn. · Kibbutz Kinneret · Kinneret Jn. · 92

767 · Deganya Alef · Tel Katsir

Yavne'el · Alumot · Yardenit · Ma'agan · Ma'agan Jn.

Deganya Bet · Tsemakh Jn. · Khamat Gader Jn.

90 · Sha'ar ha-Golan · 98

Beit Zara · Masada

Afikim

1 Casanova Guesthouse
2 Ein Gev Holiday Resort
3 Arbel B&B

TOUR 5 SNAPSHOT

Looking at the map of Tour 5, the Jordan River flows into the Sea of Galilee from the north near Bethsaida and then flows out of the lake on its southern end at Yardenit.

The Sea of Galilee sits between the northern and southern sections of the Jordan River.

The tour can begin at either end. Both end with the Jordan River.

Sites
Bethsaida, Korazim, Kursi, Susita, Jordan River, Yardenit

Length
Plan at least a full day for all the sights in the tour. Those using public transportation might have to shorten visits, especially if Susita is included.

Type
All sites are easy walking tours except for a small climb at Kursi. If you choose to hike up Susita it is a steep 4 km.

Highlights
The opportunity to actually enter the Jordan River for many pilgrims is one of the highlights of a Holy Land tour. Remember to bring a bathing suit!

The view of the Sea of Galilee from the ruined chapel at Kursi is famous. Don't miss the fish carved in stone at the synagogue at Korazim.

TOUR 5 INTRODUCTION

Jesus began his ministry in the Jordan River and during his three years of teaching and working miracles, Jesus rarely left the confines of Galilee. He crossed the border into the area of direct Roman rule, the Decapolis, where the miracle of the swine took place.

Jesus began his ministry with the Jordan, like his previous namesake Joshua Ben Nun who led the children of Israel into the Promised Land across the Jordan. Later Jesus took his message to the Gentiles—to all of mankind when he charged the Gergesene demonic,

> *"Go home to your own people and tell them how much the Lord has done for you, and how he has had mercy on you." So the man went away and began to tell in the Decapolis how much Jesus had done for him. And all the people were amazed."*
>
> Mark 5:19-20

Jesus began his transformation from a Jewish leader and prophet and opened up his message to the whole world.

These world-shaping events happened here in a backwater of the world's greatest empire at that time—Rome. Jesus' message, which at first was directed towards his own people, made its way to the heart of the empire and the world was never the same again.

Visiting Bethsaida/Jordan River Park

Hours
Open 7 days a week
☎ 04-692-3422

Entance Fee
Free if you walk or bike in (you can rent a bike from hostels in Tel Aviv & Tiberias.) Parking: 55NIS per vehicle; 70NIS for an overnight visit. Basic camping area.

How to Get There
By car, from the south go north on Route 90. At Capernaum Junction, turn right onto Route 87. Follow this until Bethsaida Junction, Route 888. Turn left here. The site of Bethsaida will be a few hundred meters north on your left. From the north: take route 90 south until the light of Almagor Junction. Make a left here and then another left at Route 8277. Take this to the end of the road and turn left on Route 87. Another left on Route 888 and the park, 1 km down, is on your left.

By bus, take bus 15 from Tiberias and get off at Yehudiya Junction. A 2.5 km walk (about 30 minutes) to the park will be necessary. Three afternoon buses; 45 min; 20NIS.

JORDAN RIVER

During the high-priesthood of Annas and Caiaphas, the word of God came to John son of Zechariah in the wilderness. He went into all the country around the Jordan, preaching a baptism of repentance for the forgiveness of sins. As it is written in the book of the words of Isaiah the prophet:

"A voice of one calling in the wilderness,
'Prepare the way for the Lord,
  make straight paths for him.
Every valley shall be filled in,
  every mountain and hill made low.
The crooked roads shall become straight,
  the rough ways smooth.
And all people will see God's salvation.'"

Luke 3:2-6

Many pilgrims are disappointed when they first see the Jordan River. Mark Twain, author and former river pilot, was surprised to find a mere stream when he expected something grander than his old stomping grounds in Mississippi. Twain wrote "...many streets in America are double as wide than the Jordan."

Yes, the Jordan River is small. Rarely is it more than 13 m (43 ft) across. From Yardenit on the southern end of the Sea of Galilee to where it empties into the Dead Sea, the Jordan meanders about 135 km (84 mi).

The Jordan gets its name from its main tributary, the Dan Springs. Yarden, the Hebrew word for the Jordan, comes from "Yored HaDan"—the Dan descends. The other two tributaries of the Jordan are the Banias (Hermon) Springs and the Hatzbani (Snir) which together make up about half of the river, with the other half coming from the Dan Springs.

TRADITIONAL BAPTISM SITE: QASR AL YAHUD

Though not in the regional scope of this book, the traditional site of Jesus' baptism by John is still worth a mention. Qasr Al Yahud ("Palace of the Jew") is located in the Palestinian Territories near Jericho and not far from Qumran National Park. Qumran became famous in the middle of the 20th century as the place where the Dead Sea Scrolls were found.

When the site was excavated by the French Institute of Biblical Archaeology in Jerusalem, it was assumed that the Jews who lived at Qumran were the authors of the scrolls found nearby. More interesting was that those Jews were none other than the third sect of Judaism mentioned by the Jewish historian Flavius Josephus in his writings, the **Essenes**.

Hence, many scholars have proposed that John was, at one time, an Essene. This is intriguing, because the Essenes built an elaborate system of Jewish ritual baths, mikva (pl. mikva'ot) even though Jews at that time (150 BCE to 68 CE) usually went to the mikva to ensure ritual purity to worship at the Temple in Jerusalem.

The Essenes negated the Temple in Jerusalem. As it was corrupt, they wanted to build a new Temple—a new Jerusalem! They wanted to purify the body as renewing the spirit's dedication to the Almighty.

The baptismal site at Qasr El Yahud (Bethany-beyond-the-Jordan) was very convenient, as it was close to Jerusalem and Jericho and was relatively easy to get to by Byzantine pilgrims.

One of the best reference books in English to be published recently on the subject of biblical geography is *The Sacred Bridge: Carta's Atlas of the Biblical World* by Anson F. Rainey and R. Steven Notley.

The Israel Nature and Parks Authority is planning on opening Qasr El Yehud to the general public in the near future. As this book went to press, visits were only arranged through tour operators and guides.

Narrow and shallow it may be, but its importance in the Bible is monumental. Moses never crossed the Jordan into the promised land, but his successor Joshua lead the children of Israel across, (Joshua 3-4) marking the spot with twelve stones to represent each of the tribes. With this "baptism," the children of Israel were reborn a nation in their own land.

The great prophets of Israel, Elijah and Elisha crossed the Jordan. Just before he ascends to heaven in a "chariot of fire," Elijah struck the waters to pass over (2 Kings 2:8). Broken hearted, the prophet Elisha did the same (2 Kings 2:14) with Elijah's mantle and "the spirit of Elijah rest[ed] on Elisha".

Naaman was told by Elisha that his leprosy would be healed if he washed himself in the Jordan (2 Kings 5:14-15). Thus the Jordan held salvation not only for Israel, but for Gentiles, too.

The Gospel of Mark begins with John the Baptist "preparing the way." Clearly alluding to Elijah, John wants to cleanse the people of Israel from sin. He wanted them to rededicate themselves.

This was a radical departure of ritual purity at that time. When the Temple in Jerusalem was standing, ritual cleansing was performed in a river, sea, lake or mikvah bath. The purpose was to remove impurity to enable the individual to worship in a ritually pure state at the Temple in Jerusalem.

John is not interested in just ritual purity, but in the individual to rededicate themselves to be better Jews, to be better to one another, and to live better lives.

What better place for Israel to renew itself than the Jordan! As Joshua led the children of Israel into the promised land and redemption, Jesus will lead all humankind to redemption.

BETHSAIDA & JORDAN RIVER PARK

Combining the Hebrew Bible (the ancient city in Geshur) and Christian scripture, Bethsaida offers a great starting point. Start the day in the cool of the morning with a walk through the excavations and enjoy a picnic snack next to the Jordan. If you are so inclined, treat yourself to a leisurely ride down the Jordan at Abu Kayak.

Perhaps the site with the most "bang for your buck," offering:

1. An archaeological park
2. Camping grounds
3. Three different hiking trails
4. Kayak boat excursions—row your boat on the Jordan

A house in Bethsaida that may have belonged to one of the disciples.

After paying your entrance fee, ask for a map of the site. As of this printing, the map is only in Hebrew, but the hiking trails are color coded. Following the trails, you can read the individual signs in English that point out the main attractions.

JESUS' BAPTISM IN THE JORDAN RIVER

At that time Jesus came from Nazareth in Galilee and was baptized by John in the Jordan. Just as Jesus was coming up out of the water, he saw heaven being torn open and the Spirit descending on him like a dove. And a voice came from heaven: "You are my Son, whom I love; with you I am well pleased."

Mark 1:9-11

The Gospels of Mark and John begin with Jesus' baptism by John.

Most Christian scholars place this site at "Bethany beyond the Jordan" (meaning on the eastern Jordanian bank) just a few kilometers north of where the Jordan River empties into the Dead Sea near Jericho. The site is called **Qasr El Yahud** ("palace of the Jews"; see sidebar on p. 149). Tradition also says this site was where Joshua crossed the Jordan when he led Israel into Canaan (Joshua 3:16), where 12 stones, representing the 12 tribes, were placed as a memorial on the river's bank.

Rainey and Notley, two of the world's leading Christian scholars, believe that the site is not in the Jordan Valley, but north of the Sea of Galilee near the town of **Bethsaida**. The wilderness that Mark speaks of as the base of operations for John is the pastureland in the lowlands of today's Golan Heights.

The Jordan River, with its headwaters just south of the Hermon Mountain in the Golan Heights, runs south, emptying into the Sea of Galilee. Then from the very southern tip of the lake, the river runs south, finally spilling into the Dead Sea.

These two scholars base their theory on the ritual purity of the Jordan River. The lower Jordan, which leaves the Sea of Galilee from the southern part of the lake, is joined by another river, the Yarmuk, a few kilometers downstream. According to 1st-century rabbis, this fusion of rivers rendered the Jordan impure for ritual immersion. John would have been extremely sensitive to this and might have performed his ablutions above the point where the Yarmuk joins the Jordan. That would probably be in the Upper Jordan on the very northern end of the lake because Mark says that John was "in the wilderness" (Mark 1:4). This does not necessarily mean that John was in the desert north of the Dead Sea, but in an uninhabited pastureland (*eremos* in Greek). This might seem to rule out the southern Yardenit site of today, but can we be sure?

> *When the apostles returned, they reported to Jesus what they had done. Then he took them with him and they withdrew by themselves to a town called Bethsaida, but the crowds learned about it and followed him. He welcomed them and spoke to them about the kingdom of God, and healed those who needed healing.*
>
> Luke 9:10-11

Though not one of the best preserved of any of the cities mentioned in Galilee, I think Bethsaida warrants a visit.

Bethsaida, which means "the house (place) of hunting or fishing," dates from the time of Jesus. Herod's son Philip, who inherited the Golan (Gaulanitis) from his father, renamed the city Julias, after the late emperor Augustus' wife, Livia-Julia, and making it a polis, a city with its own governing council. Philip liked the place so much, he was buried here, according to Josephus.

And he took (the apostoles) and withdrew apart to a city called Bethsaida. When the crowds learned it, they followed him; and he welcomed them and...cured those who need of healing. Luke 9:10

Bethsaida is important in the New Testament (it is one of only three towns on the lake mentioned), but being home to at least three of the disciples, Simon Peter, Andrew and Philip, is not its only claim to fame.

Known as the city of Zer on the Sea of Galilee, the town fell into the territory of Geshur, which was under King David's sway. Its king, Talmai, gave his daugher Maachah to David as a bride. Their son, Absalom, escaped to Geshur, after killing his half-brother Amnon for raping Absalom's sister, Tamar (2 Samuel 13).

Absalom stayed two years in Geshur. Was he residing here at Bethsaida at any part of that time?

Zer was destroyed along with most of the Kingdom of Israel in the Assyrian conquest in 732 BCE.

First identified in modern times by the American missionary and Bible scholar Edward Robinson[1] in 1838, the locals referred to it as e-Tell ("the mount" in Arabic). "Bethsaida" means "house of the fishermen" in Hebrew. Rabbi Yeshua (as Jesus would have been called by the locals 2,000 years ago) performed some of his most important miracles near here: the feeding of the multitudes, healing of a blind man and, of course, walking on the water of the nearby Sea of Galilee.

However, if this is Bethsaida, a village of fishermen, why is it almost a mile from the shore?

Apparently, the shore was much closer 2,000 years ago, as the lake covered more area than today. Also, the small port on the beach would have been located a few hundred meters from the main part of the village. This would have been done to avoid the bad smell of the dead fish and the accompanying flies and other pests.

BETHSAIDA HISTORIC SITE

Turn left as you enter the park and follow signs to the excavation.

The site is very well-marked with signs that give an explanation of each find. Park your car next to the bathrooms and follow the path up the hill. You will see a low, modern basalt wall with concrete patching it. This was a Syrian military stronghold before 1967. Minefields still surround the road here, so stick to the marked paths. Don't take the first path right, but continue straight up the hill until you see the first stone marker.

---

1 The remains of a huge arched stairway on the western wall of the Temple Mount in Jerusalem bears his name, as he was the first one to correctly identify it as the southernmost entrance to the Temple by the west

Not much remains of Bethsaida.[2] The winemaker's house and the fisherman's house have very good illustrations marking them. Note that the buildings are all built from local basalt stone.

The path comes to an end with a shaded area with stone markers that point to important sites in the Galilee such as Capernaum, Korazim, etc.

Walk back to the car park the way you came. If you are here in the summer and the dig is in full swing, I highly recommend striking up a conversation with some of the volunteers. New discoveries are often made, and you just might witness something really special!

You can now go back to the main road and turn left. The road ends with the Abu Kayak rides area. Here you can have a ride or have a walk along the Jordan. Just follow the road with the Abu Kayak site to your left and you'll come to a sign with the three

---

2   The site is currently being dug by Dr. Rami Arav of the University of Nebraska, Omaha. Should you want to volunteer for the dig in the summer, go to www.unomaha.edu/bethsaida and apply online.

routes marked in yellow, red and blue. Take the yellow route, which takes about 1 hour and 15 minutes. You'll see the Jordan and historic flour mills on the way.

KORAZIM NATIONAL PARK

Not far from Bethsaida is the northernmost point of the "holy triangle" of Jesus' ministry, Korazim. Most tours don't stop here, but lately the park has more and more pilgrims arriving to see the secret of the synagogue.

Then Jesus began to denounce the towns in which most of his miracles had been performed, because they did not repent. "Woe to you, Chorazin! Woe to you, Bethsaida! For if the miracles

Visiting Korazim National Park

Hours
8am to 5pm (Apr-Sept); to 4pm (Oct-Mar)
☎ 04-693-4982

Entrance Fee
21NIS for adults; 9NIS for youth aged 5-17.

How to Get There
By car, from Tiberias, take Route 90 north and before Amiad Junction turn right on Route 8277. From the north, drive south on Route 90 and turn left at Amiad Junction. Another left at route 8277 to the National Park.

By bus, from Tiberias, buses 841, 840, 963, and 63 can drop you off at Korazim Junction. From there, it's a 2.5 kilometer walk to the entrance. 25 min, 15.4NIS.

Kayaking down the Jordan River near Bethsaida.

The gable of the Synagogue at Korazin. The eagle's chest feathers are just under the keystone on top. The fish is located on the stone to the left of the keystone.

> *that were performed in you had been performed in Tyre and Sidon, they would have repented long ago in sackcloth and ashes.*
> Matthew 11:20-21 (See also Luke 10:13)

In the first century CE, both Korazin and Bethsaida were Jewish villages, while Tyre and Sidon were Gentile. Jesus expressed his anger at the unwillingness of the inhabitants (Jews, not Gentiles) to truly change their ways.

We know where Korazim existed. The site was excavated by Zeev Yeiven, among others, but the ruins you see in front of you are mostly from the Byzantine period (4th through 7th centuries CE).

The town Jesus knew was the acropolis, on a hill north of the park. It has yet to be excavated.

Though Korazim was famous for its wheat, which was used for first-fruit offerings in the Temple in Jerusalem, it was also a fishing village, as evidenced by the fact fishing implements were found in the excavations. Fishermen lived here as late as the 16th century.

Korazim is worth a visit because of two things:

The first is the 4th-century CE synagogue with its beautiful friezes[3]. One frieze of particular interest shows a fish.

Fishermen

A fisherman at the time of Jesus was just one cut above a beggar. Their standing was of a "hired-hand." Since they had no land, and little stake in this world, Jesus' message of "the last shall be first and the first shall be last" would have seemed particularly appealing.

Fish

Ichthus (IXΘYC) in Greek, is an acronym. The letters in the word stood for: Iesous (Jesus) CHistos (Christ) THeou (God) Uiou (Son) Soter (Savior)

On the gable which stood over the entrance of the synagogue was an eagle. Its head and wings were destroyed by iconoclasts, but to the eagle's right, carved in the basalt stone and perfectly visible to the worshippers as they entered if they looked directly above them, was one of the earliest symbols of Christians, a fish.

Fish are almost nonexistent in early synagogues in the Galilee and Golan. The fish here looks as if it was added later, not part of the original decoration.

---

3   A frieze is a decorated horizontal band on top of a wall, usually below an ornamental molding called a cornice.

The fish on the entrance of the synagogue at Korazin. A secret code symbol for Judeo-Christians?

We know that Judeo-Christians[4] did exist in the region of Israel and were not exactly welcomed by the Jewish sages of the time.

Is the synagogue at Korazim a Judeo-Christian synagogue? Would that also explain the enigmatic human carvings on the lintels?

When visiting the synagogue, note the "Moses Chair" next to the north entrance. Like in synagogues today, this seat of honor was for the person who donated monies for its building. The floral designs chiseled into the basalt rock are particularly impressive.

---

4   Judeo-Christians were Jews who accepted Jesus as the Messiah.

(This is a replica—the original is in the newly renovated Israel Museum in Jerusalem).

The second reason to visit is just to get a feel of a Galilean village at the time of Jesus. To the east of the synagogue is a complex of buildings. A paved central courtyard is surrounded on the south, east and west with buildings, all of which have a doorway leading out into the courtyard.

Here, perhaps, is a good place to take out the Bible, open it to one of Jesus' parables and read. In a place like this, Jesus would have come and found an audience of poor fishermen and their families, thirsting to know of a better world that awaits them. Was this man the Messiah? The long-awaited "offshoot of Jesse" who would deliver them from the tyrannical Roman rule?

Before leaving, note the Jewish mikveh, used in the centuries following Jesus' death. Most of the year it is filled with water.

On the return trip to the Sea of Galilee, be sure to take Route 8277 (right turn out of the park) down. There are marked car parks that take full advantage of the magnificent vistas of the lake and surrounding area.

A model of the Moses chair at Korazim.

KURSI NATIONAL PARK

The demons begged Jesus, "Send us among the pigs; allow us to go into them." He gave them permission, and the impure spirits came out and went into the pigs. The herd, about two thousand in number, rushed down the steep bank into the lake and were drowned.

Mark 5:12-13

We are now not in Antipas' Kingdom of the Galilee. Two thousand years ago, this part of the world was the Decapolis. The Decapolis was a loose confederation of ten cities (Beit Shean, then called Scythopolis-Nysa, was the capital) situated in present-day Syria, Northern Israel and Jordan. Kursi, then called "the region of the Gerasenes" or "Gedarenes," was at the most northern part of

Visiting Kursi

Hours: 8am-5pm Apr-Sept, 8am-4pm Oct-Mar; Fridays park closes one hour earlier.
☎ 04-673-1983

Entrance Fee: 14NIS for adults; 7NIS for children

How to Get There
By car, from Capernaum go east on Route 87 to where it intersects with Route 92. Turn south on Route 92 and drive for about 10 km. Kursi will be on your left with good signage in English.

By bus, from Tiberias bus 15, 18 or 22 go around the southern end of the Sea of Galilee and up the eastern shore. Get off at Kursi Junction, a few hundred meters from the site entrance. Runs from noon to 7:10 pm on weekdays; 30 min.

the Decapolis. Just to the other side of the dry river bed of Nahal Samahk was the kingdom of Herod's son Philip, called Gaulinitis—today's Golan Heights.

Scripture is unclear as to where the miracle of the swine took place. Some scholars say the miracle happened in Gedara, situated at the very southern tip of the lake. Others in Gerasa or Jerash, which is in present-day Jordan and boasts fantastic Roman ruins and is more than 40 km inland!

How do we decide where the event took place? Common sense and knowledge of geography of the Holy Land places the event where the early Christians placed it: here at Kursi.

Kursi is on the lake near enough for Jesus' boat to get blown ashore here. The area was predominantly Gentile, as evidenced by the presence of pigs in the story.

However, you usually can't go wrong with the old adage, "holy places stay holy." There is a reason the largest Byzantine monas-

The Church at Kursi. The possessed man's cave is on the mountainside above.

tery was built here. Local Jewish-Christians and later converted believers would have kept the memory of the miracle alive: passed from father to son (and/or mother to daughter) until Byzantine Christian authorities deemed the site appropriate to build a structure to commemorate the event which is mentioned in three of the four gospels.

The site was discovered in 1970, in the process of paving a new highway around the lake. In four seasons of excavations between 1970 and 1974, the walled monastery, the church, bathhouse, and other remains were discovered. The excavated monastery was huge: a square wall, 120x140 m (394x460 ft), protected the monks.

The wall you see on your left as you enter the site was covered with a light colored plaster and decorated with floral designs.

The entrance we use today to get to the church was actually the main entrance into the compound. The church must have been

בית בד
OLIVE
PRESS

magnificent. At 25x45 m (82x148 ft), it was one of the largest in the Holy Land. Like the church at Tabgha, it has a large atrium. Those aren't wells, but two openings from which water was drawn out from a large cistern underneath where you a standing. It was filled with rain water.

Before walking in the main hall, go to the right (north) and look at the olive press. Notice the large millstones which were used to crush the olives into a paste. This process of crushing the fruit usually lasted about thirty minutes.

The paste was put into doughnut-shaped baskets which were stacked on the press. Pressure was then applied to extract the oil. The earlier the pressing, the better the oil.

Leave the olive press and enter the church. The main hall (nave)[5] is bare, but at one time was covered with a mosaic. The side aisles are covered with a beautiful mosaic design. Notice that some of the mosaics are damaged. This was not due to the ravages of time,

---

5   The word "nave" comes from the Latin navis which means ship. This is because the ceiling of a church looked like the inside of the hull of a ship.

OLIVE OIL

"Virgin" olive oil, the first and best to consume, is called "virgin" in honor of the Greek goddess Athena, to whom the olive tree was sacred. In ancient Athens, heros and Olympic champions were given crowns of olive branches. The city was named after her. Her most important gift to man was the olive tree, which gave him shade the summer, oil to nourish when hungry and light to illuminate the night.

A mosaic at Kursi with natural and geometric motifs.

but Muslim iconoclasts who destroyed images of animals so they could use the building for religious purposes, as they regarded these representations of humans and animals as idolatrous.

Interestingly, some of these pictures represent baskets with bread and fish fins. Perhaps these are the remains of the feeding of the 4,000 (Mark 8:1-9 and Matthew 15:32-39), which tradition places nearby at Tel Hadar?

At the end of the main hall is an apse. Note that it is elevated over the main floor. On either side of the apse are two rectangular rooms. The one on the right (south) was converted into a baptistry in 585 CE. We know the year by the Greek inscription at the entrance. It says that the baptistry floor was paved when the monastery was ruled by the Abbot Stephanos and in the reign of the Byzantine emperor Mauricius.

On the far right hand side of the basilica (if you are facing the apse) are two chapels. The western one (nearer the entrance to the church) served as a *diaconicon*—a place where vestments, divine books, etc. that were used in the service were kept. Under you is a crypt that contained six burial troughs where important clergy were laid to rest.

Leaving the basilica, a path on the left leads up to a chapel on the hillside. Situated 200 m southeast of the church, the chapel was built around the mouth of the possessed man's cave.

The cave and most of the chapel have been destroyed by earthquakes and invasions through the ages. What appears to be a large stone gumdrop is probably the remains of a column that supported the roof of the cave. Though not a lot remains of this chapel, Christian graffiti and remains of a mosaic floor can still be seen.

Early Christian pilgrim graffiti at Kursi.

SUSITA

Susita (Aramaic) and its Greek name Hippos both mean "horse." The name apparently derives from the fact that the city sitting astride the hill reminded one of a rider on a horse.

Founded sometime between the 4th and 2nd century BCE, the Gentile city was removed from Jewish rule by the Roman general Pompey the Great in 64 BCE. He placed the city in the Decapolis, a loose federation of ten cities under Roman rule. The cities importance was due to the fact that it lay on the main road between Beth Shean, the capital of the Decapolis, and Damascus.

Rarely visited by foreign tourists, Susita boasts four churches, an olive and wine press, paved roads and magnificent views of the Sea of Galilee, the Golan and the surrounding area.

View of the Sea of Galilee from Susita in spring.

Visiting Susita

How to Get There

Route 92 begins at the very northeast corner of the Sea of Galilee on Route 87 east. Continue until you pass the entrance of Kibbutz Ein Gev.

By car, the unmarked road begins about 300 m south of the entrance on the opposite side of the road. The 3.5 km drive up is breathtaking. Park the car at the green national park sign.

By foot, a steep 4 km trail begins behind Ein Gev and takes about 1 hour. Bring plenty of water in hot weather. The trail is marked black. Be sure not to go into unmarked areas as there are old minefields here!

YARDENIT BAPTISMAL SITE

The baptism site at Yardenit is probably not the historical spot where John baptized Jesus. However, it is the Jordan River and it is in the Holy Land.

For $6, you can rent a white robe to wear in the water (a bathing suit underneath is a must) and receive a baptismal certificate (restrooms and changing room included).

If you plan to do a group baptism, please contact the site to reserve an area ahead of time. Yardenit can also film your group baptism and will cut a CD on the spot for about $15.

Visiting Yardenit Baptismal Site

Hours
Open daily 8am to 5pm (Oct 1-March 31); to 6pm (April 1-Sep 30).

☎ 04-675-9111

Entrance
Free. Small fee for restrooms.

How to Get There
The Yardenit site is conveniently located just off Route 90 just a few kilometers south of Tiberias. Closed only on the Jewish day of atonement, Yom Kippur. Closes an hour earlier on Fridays.

By bus, buses 961, 28, 15, 18, 19, 22 and 24 from Tiberias can let you off at Yardenit, 10 min. From Nazareth, bus 31 goes to Yardenit, a journey of about an hour.

www.yardenit.com

Baptism in the Jordan River is a highlight for many pilgrims

WHERE TO STAY:

Tiberias makes a convenient, if not very inspired, base for travel around the Sea of Galilee. If you have a car, I recommend sleeping at one of the many rural B&Bs and guesthouses outside of urban centers.

Casa Nova Franciscan Guesthouse
(☎04-671-2281; Ha Yarden St; casanova@koinoniagb.org)
The Franciscans brothers run this clean, simple and inexpensive guesthouse close to St. Peter's Church in downtown Tiberias.

Scots Hotel
(☎04-671-0710; 1 Gdud Barak Street; www.scotshotels.co.il)
For luxury accommodations, this place is unbeatable. A former Scottish hospital, this boutique hotel offers beautiful historic grounds including an "archaeological walk" through Roman and Byzantine ruins.

Ein Gev Holiday Resort
(☎04-665-8008; www.eingev.com)
On the eastern shore of the Sea of Galilee, Kibbutz Ein Gev runs popular tourist services including hotel and apartment accommodations, a beach campground, tourist boats and a famous fish restaurant.

Arbel B&B
(☎04-6794919, Moshav Arbel, www.4shavit.com)
Sara and Israel Shavit run a charming guesthouse in Arbel village, just 10 minutes from Tiberias by car. Features comfortable suites, a swimming pool, and a highly-rated restaurant featuring the specialty of the house—lamb casserole. Reasonable prices and relaxing atmosphere.

SIDE TRIP:
DAN & CAESAREA PHILIPI

The Dan spring is the largest in the Middle East, yielding more than 250 million m³ of water a year! The Banias spring is less ambitious with an annual output of about half that, at 125 million m³, which makes up 25% of the Jordan River. The remainder comes from the third main tributary of the Jordan, the Snir (Hatzbani).

The time of Jesus was a very dangerous time to be popular in the region of Israel. Herod Antipas (the "fox") ruled the Galilee. His father, Herod the Great, had divided his kingdom between three of his sons upon his death. Archelaus,[1] his oldest surviving son, inherited Judea, Idumaea and Samaria. Philip, the youngest of the three, received Gaulauntis (today's Golan Heights and northwest Jordan).

If Herod "the Great" had taught his sons anything, it was to mercilessly crush anyone that might threaten their rule over their kingdoms. John the Baptist sealed his fate when he spoke out against the marriage of Herod Antipas to Herodias, Antipas' niece (which John correctly asserted was against Mosaic law). Stirring the people against a Herodian was suicidal. He was put to death at Machaeus, one of Herod's desert fortresses on the eastern side of the Jordan.

Jesus is acutely aware that he cannot attract too much attention. Heeding the adage "out of sight, out of mind," he and his disciples set off to the very fringe of Philip's jurisdiction outside of his capital Caesarea Philipi, the site of the Banias or Hermon Spring.

---

1   Herod executed three of his sons and had his beloved wife Miriamne murdered. It is said that Caesar Augustus quipped, "It is safer to be Herod's pig than his son." (Herod abstained from eating pork, following Jewish kashruth laws).

Visiting Tel Dan National Park

Hours
8am to 5pm, Oct-March park closes 1 hour earlier. Last entry 1 hour before closing
☎ 04-695-1579

Entrance Fee
Adults/children 27/14NIS

How to Get There
Drive north on Route 90. Drive through the small town of Kiryat Shmoneh. Turn east on Route 99. Follow the signs to the park entrance. It is possible, but unwieldy, to travel to Dan by bus.

When Jesus came to the region of Caesarea Philippi, he asked his disciples, "Who do people say the Son of Man is?" They replied, "Some say John the Baptist; others say Elijah; and still others, Jeremiah or one of the prophets."

"But what about you?" he asked. "Who do you say I am?" Simon Peter answered, "You are the Messiah, the Son of the living God."
Matt 16:13-16

HERMON SPRINGS (BANIAS)

The Banias waterfall is a must see and is on the way (on Route 99) to the main entrance of the site. Your entrance fee is good to enter both, so hang onto the receipt.

After parking your car (if you haven't arrived on foot), follow the path that leads up to the large karstic cave above you. You will go over the springs on your way there.

The Romans believed that such a place was invariably inhabited by demi-gods or nymphs. "Banias" is an Arabic pronunciation of the word "Paneon"—the city of Pan. (The Arabic alphabet does not contain the letter P, so the letter B is often substituted).

Herod builds his city dedicated to the local cult of Pan and also to show tribute to his patron, Augustus Caesar. He foots the bill for the construction of a large temple to both. Wait a minute, a Jewish King building pagan temples?

Herod is king of the Jews, but does not identify himself with Jews. He comes from pagan stock. He never feels comfortable in Jewish company. No fool, Herod builds his city on the crossroads of three important routes: 1) the Via Patris linking Egypt with Damascus; 2) the spur of same road that goes west to Tyre (the Via Maris) and 3) the road to the Tigris.

Banias Springs - Watch your step when crossing them! I suggest starting with the springs, which are further north than the waterfall.

When walking up to the very scant remains of the large temple complex built by Herod, a white-domed structure sits on the mountain to your left. This is a tomb of the Wali[2] el-Hader, (St. George) holy to the Druze, Muslims and Christians alike.

The god Pan had the legs of a goat and a reputation among the ladies. One young creature named Echo had a child by him but was unlucky enough to fall in love with Narcissus. He rejected her, and she pined away until the only thing left were her words.

Goats were sacrificed to the god Pan by the locals here and also apparently there was a bit of a "floor show." When Christianity was "decriminalized" by Constantine in the 4th century, the other pagan shrines had to resort to light entertainment to keep their worshippers from turning to this new religion.

---

2   "Wali" is the Arabic for a saint or holy person.

Visiting Banias Nature Reserve

Hours
8am to 5pm (April-September)
8am to 4pm (October-March).
No entrance within one hour of closing time.

Entrance Fee
Adult 27NIS; child 14NIS

How to Get There
Take Route 99 from Kiryat Shmona east. Banias lies 3 km east of Kibbutz Snir. The Hermon Springs Nature Reserve has two entrances connected by a hiking trail. You don't have to hike the trail to get to both sites.

Here at Caesarea Philipi, the priests trained goats to dance and held shows for the "tourists." Now I have never seen a goat dance, so it must have been a prime attraction in these parts!

The short trail returns you to the souvenir shop. You can return to your car or continue to one of the three hiking trails that originate at the same point. Walk past the shop and continue straight past pools of fresh spring water with fish in them that pass an ancient water-driven flour mill, the Banias (Hermon) stream, and the ruins of the capitol of Agrippa II with synagogue and vaulted storage rooms. It takes about an hour and is definitely worth the effort in most weather.

The second option is to take the longer trail that leads to the Banias waterfall. Not recommended in summer months, this hike takes about one and a half to two hours. The waterfall at the end is spectacular and the route quite lovely as well.

The less ambitious can return to their car. Leave the park by driving south (right) on Route 99 and backtracking to the entrance of the Banias waterfall, which will be on your left.

Here there are two options: the first is a ten minute walk down some steep stairs that will lead you to one of the two perennial waterfalls in Israel.

However, the second and **must do** option is the take the new "suspended bridge" trail that opened in April 2010. The trailhead boasts "the most beautiful trail in Israel" and they just might be right! The sound of the rushing waters and the magnificent sight of the white water racing south to join the Jordan River will be one of the highlights of your trip. Keep following the red trail marker until you reach the waterfall.

PLANNING YOUR TRIP TO THE GALILEE

WHEN TO GO

Unlike most of North America and Europe, Israel does not have four "true" seasons.

There are two main seasons—winter and summer. The rainy season (winter) lasts from about mid-October to mid-March, and the dry season (summer) from mid-May to the end of September. The two "transitional" seasons, spring and fall, can be cold and rainy, but due to "off-season" hotel rates and few crowds at tourist sites, these can be the best times to visit.

However, the best time to come to the Galilee is in the short spring season, about the last two weeks in March. The hills and valleys are filled with wild flowers, the weather is mild and the views are simply fantastic.

The "false fall" as I call it, is from October to the first week or two of December. It's also a great time to visit. Hotels tend to be fairly empty and so are the sites, but rainy weather might interfere. Summer is convenient for students, but it does get very hot, especially from the beginning of July to mid-September.

Be warned! Keep away during the Jewish Passover holiday. The Jewish calendar is lunar (with a solar-adjusted leap year) so the date of Passover always changes. Go online and check out when the Jewish Passover

holiday is. It lasts seven days in Israel. You can spend most of your trip stuck in hours-long traffic jams and the sites are sometimes closed due to overcrowding! Hotels are jammed and very expensive. There's not a large selection to eat because of the proscription against eating leavened foods. Lots of foods (all breads, rolls, beer, etc.) aren't available.

Stay away unless you're staying with friends or relatives. If you risk it and get to overcrowded, litter-strewn sites in national parks, don't say that I didn't warn you!

WHAT TO TAKE

Twice the money and half the clothes doesn't cut it here. Since you will be visiting holy sites, archaeological parks and city centers, a good pair of thick-soled walking shoes is a must. Sneakers, running shoes or trainers tend to slip on wet limestone and don't do that great of a job supporting your feet.

A good hat is a must, preferably one that covers the nape of your neck and has UV protection. Tilley® hats seem to do the trick, as do ones made by Columbia Sportswear®, North Face® and Outdoor Research.® Hydration should be on your mind. Drink lots of water. Consider buying a water bottle with strap.

Needless to say, comfortable clothes that fit the season are something everyone will take. Long slacks or skirts and shirts with sleeves and collar are almost always more practical than shorts and t-shirts. Many holy sites prohibit shorts and sleeveless shirts on both men and women. Longer clothes keep you warmer and provide sun protection. Hiking sandals like Source,® Teva® or Chaco® may come in handy. A good rule of thumb is to cover your knees and shoulders when visiting religious sites in Israel.

Definitely bring a good sunblock. Although available for sale in the Israel, sunblock can be quite expensive.

HOW TO GET THERE

Israel has a great bus and rail system. However, most public transport doesn't run on the Jewish Sabbath (*Shabbat*). The Sabbath (see p. 189) begins an hour before sundown on Fridays and ends an hour after the sun sets on Saturday.

Buses give a discount for holders of international student IDs. Go to www.isic.org to see if you qualify. (Teachers can also get an international teacher ID, but discounts in Israel are few and far between for this noble calling).

Taxis are plentiful here, but be wary of drivers who "don't speak

English." All taxi drivers take an exam in English to get their licenses. If the driver doesn't understand you immediately, get out of the cab. For short trips, make sure they start their meter—it's a law here. For longer journeys, such as airport taxis, there are standardized flat rates.

Sheruts are privately-run system of mini buses and mini vans that run on many popular bus routes. Usually cheaper than buses and located near central bus stations, they are a great alternative. Sheruts have no fixed schedule, leave whenever they are full and run on Shabbat.

I do not recommend hitchhiking anywhere in the world. Good preparation ahead of time will save you heartache once you are here.

WHERE TO STAY

With such sites as www.tripadvisor.com and search engines such as Google, most travelers can, with a little preparation, search and book their tours online.

However, I can recommend the Kibbutz Guest House Hotel chain (www.hotels-of-israel.com/kibbutz). They are clean, friendly, efficient and reasonably priced. They lie on accessible main roads for those who will use public transportation, and are easily located for those who rent vehicles.

I especially recommend the Ginosar Village guesthouse located on the Sea of Galilee and Kibbutz Lavi in the Lower Galilee. See each tour section for specific recommendations by area.

BUDGET

Prices of flights and hotels vary greatly. Rooms in Christian hostels can be as little as $25-$40 per person per night for the Casa Nova Franciscan Pilgrim House in Tiberias to as much as $440 for a luxury suite at the Scots Hotel!

Again, taking a middle-of-the-road approach, $1,200 round-trip airfare from New York and $150 per night for a double room with breakfast, and $40 per day for food, a week's tour may cost $2,500-$3,000 per person with meals and site entrances. Transportation will vary if you rent a car or take public transportation.

Prices are based on 2011 prices, with the dollar about 3.5 to the Israeli Shekel (NIS).

CURRENCY AND CREDIT CARDS

I do not recommend walking around with a lot of cash. Keep no more than 400-500 shekels on you.. That should suffice. Be advised that traveler's checks are not honored by many establishments. The best way to obtain shekels is via an ATM cash machine. There are ATMs at Ben Gurion airport and most banks in Israeli cities have an ATM that accepts foreign cards. Let your bank know you'll be abroad so they don't suspect fraudulant charges and block any of your cards.

Credit cards (VISA, MasterCard and American Express) are honored at most businesses, but most charge a conversion fee when used for purchases in foreign currencies.

INSURANCE

Israel has a very sophisticated medical infrastructure. However, be sure to insure yourself with a reputable carrier before your trip. Many companies offer trip insurance policies, which can include emergency evacuation, trip cancellation, lost or stolen baggage, and myriad other possible complications and expenses possible when traveling.

ISRAELI ETIQUETTE

Good manners and warm customer service are not strong points of Israeli culture. Israeli-born Jews are sometimes affectionately called "sabras" after the prickly pear cactus fruit, and it is said that they are "prickly on the outside, sweet on the inside." Don't be intimidated by what may seem like a cold reception by American standards.

When standing in line, be forceful and don't let anyone cut in front of you. That's why the good Lord gave us elbows! Likewise Israeli drivers tend to be assertive and you may never get out of some intersections if you're a timid driver.

GUIDED TOURS AND TOUR GUIDES

This book is written for those who like to guide themselves. However, hiring a private guide or taking a day tour to sites like Masada, Jerusalem or the Negev greatly enhances the experience.

My website at www.guideinisrael.com is always at your service. The Jesus Trail website also offers self-guided and guided walking tours in the Galilee: www.jesustrail.com.

VISAS

US, Canadian and European Union passport holders are issued a free three-month tourist visa at the immigration desk upon arrival in Israel. Other nationalities can check with their closest embassy or consulate for visa details.

LANGUAGE

Hebrew and Arabic are the official languages of the State of Israel. Most people working in tourism have more than a passable knowledge of English.

TIME

Israel's official time zone is UTC/GMT +2, meaning seven hours ahead of the eastern US (Eastern Standard Time), and two hours ahead of the UK (Greenwich Mean Time).

CURRENCY

The New Israeli Shekel (NIS) is the official currency in Israel. Bills are 200, 100, 50 and 20 shekels respectively. (The 20 skekel bill is actually made of plastic fibers, not paper!) Coins are 10, 5, 2, 1, half shekel and 10 agarot (100 agarot = 1 shekel). Many tourist establishments and shops take dollars and euro, but know the exchange rate for that day as it can change often.

TIPPING

Service is not included in restaurants. Anywhere from 10% to 15% is recommended. Though taxi drivers don't expect tips, you can surprise them. It is customary to tip chambermaids and bellboys in hotels. 10 NIS per day for the hotel staff per day and 20 NIS to the bellboy for a families bags. If you book an organized tour, tour guides are usually tipped $5 a day per person and half that for the driver.

CAR RENTAL

You have to be at least 24 years old to rent a car in Israel and have your driver's license more than 1 year. Most foreign licenses are recognized in Israel, but getting an international driving license is always a good idea. Rental cars are usually smaller than in North

America. Rates begin at $40 per day/$200 a week for an economy model with unlimited mileage. If you want a small van or SUV, be sure to book them well ahead of time. Israeli insurance coverage will not include the Palestinian Territories. See www.hertz.co.il, www.avis.co.il or www.budget.co.il to check rates and availability.

CELL PHONES AND INTERNET

Cell phone coverage is literally everywhere (even on top of Masada). If you have a triband or quadband cell phone with place for a SIM card, you can have the phone unlocked and purchase a prepaid SIM card quite inexpensively. Roaming charges for foreign cell phone plans are often prohibitive, with charges of several dollars per minute of airtime. I suggest going to www.travelcell.com, which rents phones at reasonable rates and can even mail the phone to you before your trip. Mobile phones and SIM cards can also be purchased at the airport. The main Israeli carriers are Cellcom and Orange, which have similar costs and coverage.

Free wifi is available in almost all cafes and restaurants. Israelis don't mind you sitting and surfing for more than an hour for the cost of a latte. Ben Gurion airport offers free wifi, handy for letting friends and family know you've arrived safely or informing of any delays.

GLOBAL POSITIONING SYSTEM (GPS)

I highly recommend using a GPS if you plan to do any driving in Israel. GPS rental is available from most of the car rental companies. Smart phones and iPhone owners can purchase maps in their respective countries. A handheld GPS unit can be useful for hiking as some routes can be uploaded for foolproof navigation.

TV & NEWSPAPERS

Don't be surprised if you catch the latest House, MD or Letterman on Israeli TV. CNN, Fox News and BBC are available. *The Jerusalem Post* and *The International Herald-Tribune* are published daily.

HOLIDAYS

Remember that Saturday is the day off for most Israelis, and Sunday is a workday. Sunday is the day of prayer for Christians, so be prepared for some churches to be closed to tourists. The market and many stores in Nazareth are closed on Sundays.

Friday is a day of prayer in the Muslim sector, so some Muslim businesses may close early for Friday prayers.

As noted, remember that Passover is a difficult time to tour Israel.

On Yom Kippur, the Jewish day of atonement, the country literally shuts down. No public transportation, TV, radio. Children ride their bikes on the empty streets, as no driving is permitted.

Jewish holidays are based on the Jewish calendar, which is lunar, so go to http://urj.org/holidays/jcal/ for exact dates.

FOOD AND DRINK

Israelis love to eat. Aside from the usual pizza and hamburgers, why not try a falafel (chick peas balls served in a fresh pita with salad), shwarma (turkey or lamb meat roasted on a circular spit) or a plate of hummus?

The local wine industry has really taken off in the last 20 years. The Yarden, Yatir and Dalton labels are just a few of the many excellent wines available here. The two mainstream Israeli beers

are Maccabee and Goldstar, with smaller boutique breweries beginning to pop up. For a refreshing nonalcoholic drink, try *limonana*— lemonade blended with fresh mint leaves.

SHOPPING

You'll have plenty of opportunities for buying souvenirs. If the price is not marked on the item—bargain!

In open-air markets such as in Old City Jerusalem, bargaining is expected. Don't be surprised if the shop keeper starts at a very high rate! Counter offer with a number that is lower than than the price you actually hope to pay. If you hit a stand still, walk away and the shop keeper may come after you to accept your lower offer. You can also usually work a discount if you buy more than one of any given item.

ISRAELI NATIONAL PARKS ENTRY CARDS

Zippori is one of 67 National Parks in Israel. These sites range from nature reserves to historical ruins to hot springs, and are well-maintained with bathroom facilities and often have gift shops and snack bars. Costs for individual parks range from 10 to 30 shekels, with lower rates for children and groups of 30+ people.

If you plan to visit multiple national parks during your stay, consider purchasing a multi-entry ticket. Entrance to any six parks costs 105NIS and entrance to all parks (there are over 60!) for a two-week period costs 145NIS. Cards are good for 14 days from date of first entrance. Year-long individual or family passes are also available, which are a good value if you plan to travel longer than two weeks.

SHABBAT

The Jewish Sabbath, (*Shabbat* in Hebrew), begins about half an hour before sundown on Fridays and continues until an hour after sunset on Saturdays. In Jewish areas, most commercial businesses public transportation are closed. However, almost all tourist sites in the Galilee are still open. In Arab areas, stores are more likely to be closed on Friday and Sunday, the Muslim and Christian holy days respectively.

SUGGESTED READING

HISTORICAL JESUS

The Historical Jesus: An Essential Guide, by James H. Charlesworth, 2008.

In the Steps of Jesus, by Peter Walker, 2007.

Jesus of Nazareth, by Paula Fredriksen, 1999.

Jesus of Nazareth: His Life, Times, and Teaching, by Joseph Klausner, 1989.

The Jewish War, by Josephus, 1970.

With Jesus Through the Galilee According To The Fifth Gospel, by Bargil Pixner, 1992.

Who's Who in the Age of Jesus, by Geza Vermes, 2005.

THE HOLY LAND

The Carta Bible Atlas, by Yohanan Aharoni, 2002.

Greatness, Grace and Glory, by Paul Wright, 2008.

Hiking the Jesus Trail and Other Biblical Walks in the Galilee, by Anna Dintaman and David Landis, 2010.

The Holy Land, by Jerome Murphy-O'Connor, 2008.

The Sacred Bridge, by Anson F. Rainey and R. Steven Notley, 2006.

GENERAL BACKGROUND

Art and History of Nazareth, by Eugenio Alliata, 1995.

The Basilica of the Annunciation at Nazareth, by G.S.P. Freeman-Grenville, 1994.

The Basilica in Nazareth, by Gumbert Ludwig, 1986.

Daily Life at the Time of Jesus, by Miriam Feinberg-Vamosh, 2007.

Nazareth, by Eugenio Alliata, Metodio Brlek, Michele Piccirillo, and Bartolomeo Pirone, 1995.

The New Encyclopedia of Archaeological Excavations in the Holy Land, Efraim Stern, Editor, 1993.

Recovering Capharnaum, by Stanislao Loffreda, 1993.

The Sea of Galilee and Its Fishermen in the New Testament, by Mendel Nun, 1989.

NOTES